GOOD GRIEF

Making sense of . . .
death, dying, and funerals

by **Mark H. Shearon**

Cover Design by Ocean Vision, Redondo Beach, California
Text Design by Harold Allen Brown Graphics, Nolensville, Tennessee

Printed in the United States of America

ISBN 0-9658133-0-4

The following excerpts are reprinted with permission:

Chapter 1
The Manuscripts of Thomas D. Willhite, by Thomas D. Willhite, High Valley Ranch, Clearlake Oaks, California, pp. 108-110.

Chapter 2
A Whack on the Side of the Head, by Roger von Oech, Copyright 1983, published by Werner, Inc., p.7.

Chapter 4
Brilliant Babies, Powerful adults, by John Mike, M.D., Copyright 1996, published by Satori Press International, p.75.

Chapters 5 and 7
A Second Helping of Chicken Soup for the Soul, by Jack Canfield and Mark Victor Hansen, Copyright 1995, published by Health Communications, Inc., pp. 135,158.

Chapter 7
The Book of Comfort and Joy, "This Moment", By Paul Barnett, published by Ideals Publishing Corp., Nashville, TN, p.151.
Illusions by Richard Bach, Copyright 1977 by Creature Enterprises, Inc., published by Delacorte Press of Bantam Doubleday Dell Publishing Group, Inc., p. 121.

Throughout this book, excerpts were paraphrased from *You Were Born Rich*, by Bob Proctor, Copyright 1984, McCrary Publishing, Inc.

To:

From:

FOREWORD

This is a book that is long overdue. "Good Grief" casts a friendly light on a subject that too many people have kept hidden in the shadows of their mind. This is a book that should be in every home and used to stimulate group discussion among family members. Such discussions would prove to be one of the healthiest activities for any family.

For over three decades, I have had the good fortune of working with individuals and groups from America to Asia. This work has consisted of private and corporate consultations along with seminars where there have been anywhere from 50 to a few thousand people in the audience. The subject has always been the same: personal growth and corporate development; how to experience and enjoy life in abundance. This is something that should come naturally to us, and would, if it weren't for the layers of limitations and ignorance we must work through. It is sad but true that each of us, at birth, arrive on this planet the confluence of a genetic pool that goes back four or five generations. The doubts and fears of our parents and grandparents, unfortunately, become ours.

Death and dying, historically, have been subjects that were almost always put on the back burner to be dealt with at a later date. In most cases, it is hoped much later.

You and I have been told to "know the truth and the truth would set us free." There is only one thing to be set free from and that is ignorance. Ignorance is the only enemy you will ever have to face.

There are only two sources of reference you can go to when you are studying life or death. They are science and theology. Both of these sources clearly indicate that nothing is either created nor destroyed. That only postulates one theory which is *life*. Why then should anyone fear death? Why are we so reluctant to speak in a happy, relaxed manner about this subject? Why do we have tears of joy when a person arrives and tears of sorrow when they leave? Both life and death are a transition, a part of the eternal journey.

Theodore Roosevelt said it brilliantly when he wrote the epitaph for his son who was killed in battle, just a few months before his own passing. He wrote, "Only those are fit to live, who do not fear to die. And none are fit to die who have shrunk from the joy of life. Both life and death are part of the same great adventure. All of us who provide service and stand ready for sacrifice are the Torchbearers. We run with the torches until we fall, content if we can pass them to the hands of the other runners."

Mark Shearon is a Torchbearer. He has done a tremendous service to all in writing this book and sharing his personal experiences from early childhood to the present. He was fortunate enough to have been raised with a very healthy attitude toward a subject which is truly misunderstood by most people.

It is time to alter our perspective of death, dying and funerals, and you will before you lay this book down. Mark will bring tears to your eyes, but they will be tears of laughter.

Bob Proctor

ABOUT THE COVER

A Life Lived Is a Life Worth Celebrating
As you read this book, the cover will gain more meaning
with each chapter. Once you have finished all the chapters
of lessons as I prefer to call them, this cover can serve as a
trigger devise (a reminder) for you to think, "A Life Lived
Is a Life Worth Celebrating."

The Design
The dark clouds serve as the view most often taken when
we think about Death, Dying and Funerals.

The light beams that shine through are the light of
infinite power where we are transformed from the physical
life into the spiritual life. These beams of light serve as the
reminder that no matter how dark and dreary life seems, it
is always beautiful just beyond the clouds.

The people dancing are our reminder to celebrate.
The circle they form represents the circle of life. The center figure is a person's life that no longer exists as we think
of life in the physical form but still exists in memory. They
will never die in our hearts as long as we remember them
for the moments shared together.

The white light surrounds them as our reminder
that they have been received with open arms which sym-
bolize love, joy, and feelings that are the happiest that
could be possibly felt by anyone. There is no pain or suffering. Sadness is an absolute impossibility.

The background serves as the unending possibility
to see far beyond our past limited thoughts about Death,
Dying, and Funerals to a new vision of Good Grief.

DEDICATION

This book is dedicated to the families who gave me the opportunity to care for their loved ones, to my grandmother and grandfather for the compassion they gave so freely, to my mother and father for the guidance and healthy attitude toward death, to my wife Tina, who is the wind beneath my wings.

ACKNOWLEDGEMENT

I would like to acknowledge . . . my wife for her patience in sorting my notes into the book form that is before you and for loving me unconditionally . . . Bob Proctor for the encouragement to write about these subjects so often hidden away until it's too late – and for his guidance towards awareness of the human potential . . . Jane Willhite, co-founder of PSI Seminars, and the staff of each of the courses who offered direction to liberty and being the person I am. It was after attending those courses that I chose to make a difference in the world by writing this book.

CONTENTS

INTRODUCTION

Just sittin' around waiting for someone to die – what a horrible business! Having the grim reaper as your mascot in life can give you the "creeps." Well, it is not all bad. After all, people are dying to see me!

I have had an opportunity in my life to experience a profession that most people won't even talk about. Being born into a second generation family of funeral directors doesn't necessarily mean it's a given that a person would want to serve in this profession. My brother and sister chose not to be a part of the family business. I have been asked why I would do this for a living. After all these years in the business, the reason I did is now clear to me.

I am grateful for what I have experienced while serving the families of the deceased. I would not have my understanding and attitude about life and death without that opportunity. I am not sure I would be classified as an expert, but these experiences have made me a student of many aspects and beliefs about death. The more families I served, the more I discovered about helping them deal with the death. But even more importantly, I learned how to help them see the potential opportunities for positive and meaningful moments that too often we miss during these experiences. How we utilize these moments impacts us for the rest of our lives.

This book is meant to awaken your mind . . . to help you bring more to the experience and gain more aware-ness about yourself as you entertain ideas presented here on how to celebrate a life that was lived. Some of the material which follows may shock you at times, and you may not agree totally with all that is contained herein. Some of it will seem strange and unusual because of our society's negative concepts about death. I know you will find an opportunity to at least question your own views of death. It is my quest to open your mind and challenge you on this subject.

As you read, highlight or underline areas or the portions that interest you or make you think – especially the ones that seem to be "way out of line." As you continue to read, notice your feelings and reactions. If you begin feeling uncomfortable; be thankful. You are being challenged to change; to stretch yourself mentally and emotionally. Read this book as if it were the last day, week, or month of your earthly life.

A New Day
This is the beginning of a new day.
God has given me this day to use as I will.
I can waste it or use it for good,
But what I do today is important,
Because I am exchanging a day of my life for it.
When tomorrow comes, this day will be gone forever,
Leaving in its place something I have traded for it.
I want it to be gain and not loss,
Good, and not evil; success, and not failure,
In order that I shall not regret the price that
I have paid for it.
$$\text{\textbf{Author Unknown}}$$

. . .

Repeat this affirmation aloud:
"I give thanks today; and I now take a deep breath of release . . . letting go of every thought that is not for my highest good!"

. . .

Chapter 1

To Understand Death Is To Understand Life

Sir Winston Churchill once so aptly stated, "We make a living by what we get; we make a life by what we give." Indeed, we must first live before we can die. So many people never truly live because of their fear of dying. As a friend of mine says, "We tiptoe through life hoping to make it safely to death."

Thomas D. Willhite, a pioneer of personal growth and development in America, included in his manuscripts, "The Book of Fears." The following excerpt shares wisdom known to few:

"The fear of death is the fear of not living and not living life fully. It is the fear of being forgotten or being unimportant. It is the fear that life has no meaning. Every day we see the evidence of this fear – graphic accounts of deaths in papers and magazines, numerous TV programs involving deaths, millions spent on prolonging life (even when there is no hope of recovery), exactly following superstitions and an unknown amount spent on fortune-tellers, good luck charms, and seances . . . yet it is taboo to speak of our own death or that of a loved one. We visit the dying and reassure them that they will make it – even when we know they will not. Why do we do this? Why do so many seem more death-oriented than life-oriented? Why do we always keep death uppermost in our minds and, at the same time, push it away when it gets close? We do this, you know.

"To understand death is to understand life. Death is an integral part of life – it is the culmination of every life just as birth is the beginning. There is no avoidance, no escape. You will experience death . . . the only question is when. Are you ready for it now? It may come tomorrow. Could you go, feeling good about your life and what you left behind? If you cannot answer these questions with an unqualified, definite "yes," then is it time to start living NOW . . . NOW, this minute as you read these words? It is not too late; it is never too late. Five months of a life fully lived are worth far more than five years or even fifty of mere existence.

"I believe life is more beautiful because of death. Do we not cherish the daffodils and lilies that bloom for but a few short weeks each spring? They are more precious because they are not always with us. So it is with life. Life is more dear to us, knowing that we cannot always have it. We seek to use our time wisely, not knowing how much we have. We remember the small things – bright, sunny days, the song of a sparrow or the sound of a gentle rain – because we might not experience them again. This is as it should be. I am glad I do not know when I will die. I am glad I am forced by death to live each day in the now. My life is far richer because of death . . . and so is yours. I do not fear death, nor do I seek it. I simply am ready.

"What happens at death? I do not know. What I do know is that death is a total, individual experience. That's beautiful. Do you realize what that means? No matter what you have done in your life; no matter how heavily you have relied on others; no matter how ardently you have avoided the risks of life, YOU WILL THROUGH DEATH BE FORCED TO EXPERIENCE AND GROW ON YOUR OWN. You will be forced to stand on your own, like it or not, as all the props of material existence are stripped away. You will grow; there is no standing still in the face of death. It seems to me that the Infinite Power (God, Spirit, Truth) in its wisdom is much like a mother bird. When the time is right, the young are pushed out of the nest that they may grow strong and live in freedom. Death is that push.

"THE INFINITE IN ITS WISDOM AND LOVE HAS FORCED EACH INDIVIDUAL TO TAKE THE NEXT STEP THROUGH THE MYSTERY KNOWN AS DEATH.

"I do not find it very important to speculate on life after death or to debate reincarnation. The answers will be known to us soon enough. All that we have, all that is real, is NOW. The issue is to live fully now. That is heaven. To live in past regrets or future hopes is hell. If you would only shift your life to the NOW, you would know total happiness and freedom from fear. For to live in the NOW is to live so that there are no past regrets and no future hopes. It is to live with total individual integrity.

"TO LIVE LIFE TO THE FULLEST, LIVE EACH DAY IN TOTAL HARMONY AND INTEGRITY.

"'How do I begin?' you ask. Begin with the acceptance of death. Know that you will die, as have all people, great or small. Know, too, that this is the way life is meant to be. Death is your friend. Death is a step onward. Next ask yourself, 'What have I not done that I want to do?' Make a list of these things. Is there an old debt not settled? Is there an old hurt still festering? Is there someone you need to talk to? Are there affairs to be put in order? Have you taken steps to protect your loved ones when you cannot? Are there things you have dreamed of doing . . . tomorrow? Do all these things now, and you will have begun to live. Do one more thing, and you will be totally living. That one more thing is: to know yourself – to seek out the depths within. For those who climb the path of life in search of Truth, death is just one more step towards the goal. It is a step to be taken, not feared."

Although this book, *Good Grief*, does not have an evangelistic purpose to persuade the reader toward a religious commitment, be advised that your search for Truth and the confidence in knowing Truth, (I choose to call it God), will be the biggest key to totally living life at its fullest potential and stepping into death without fear.

. . .

Repeat this affirmation aloud:
"I greet this day with love in my heart. I am living this day as if it was my last, because life is a precious gift, and yesterday ended last night!"

"My mission in life is to unfold and grow. If this was not so, I would not be alive to be even reading these words. I now choose to unfold and grow to fulfill my true mission!"

. . .

Chapter 2
My Beginning: Rollerskating In The Casket Room

As mentioned earlier, I am the third generation of funeral directors in my family. When I look back, it amazes me that I chose this profession, realizing how it took my father away from my ballgames and other activities while I was growing up. Death has no schedule. When it comes, it demands your time and attention.

I grew up going on ambulance calls with my grandfather at the age of *eleven* in a small town on the outskirts of Nashville, Tennessee. As I look back on those days, I find it humorous to think the best means of emergency service was through the local funeral home! I thank God we were people that cared for a person's life rather than looking for the opportunity to add to the funeral business.

At the age of obtaining my driver's license (and at times prior to), I found myself and my friends making the ambulance calls. Needless to say, excitement was endless for a sixteen-year-old with a license to speed with red lights and all the newest bells and whistles (sirens). To this day, my adrenaline starts going when I hear sirens. My friends accuse me of saying, "Ah, music to my ears!"

I remember one night when we had an emergency call to go to someone's home. We were told there was an elderly person who was unconscious – possibly a heart attack. As we rushed into the house, sirens still winding down, I saw an elderly woman slumped down in a chair. I sprang into action, pulling her to the floor to a prone position, ready to begin CPR.

"Wait!!!" yelled someone. "My aunt is in the back bedroom. Granny's just sleeping!" (Whoops . . . sorry Granny.)

Getting to drive the ambulance was a bonus on top of the experience of helping people in need. Unfortunately, people would often die no matter how fast we drove or the actions we took to save their lives. I remember the one time I was in the back of the ambulance helping someone who died on the way to the hospital. It was the first time I faced death in a personal way. I had an empty feeling that I thought would never go away. The pain, grief, and intense emotions that his family had as they were told upon our arrival at the emergency room only added to my feeling of emptiness. I had never realized how devastating a person's death would be. I knew at that time there has to be a better way to deal with death than what I witnessed.

My grandparents' home also served as the funeral home. (I remember how much fun I had as a child rollerskating in the chapel and playing "hide and seek" among the caskets.) They opened their lives to the families they served. My grandmother was known to everyone in the community as "Miss Bessie." To those close to her, including me, she was known as "Mama Shearon." I remember her cooking meals for the families; sitting on the couch with members of the family, holding their hand and comforting them. In those days, she would often sit up all night with families. Her presence was a comfort to all who knew her.

My grandfather, Mr. Newton ("Big Daddy" to me), was a large-built man, and I don't remember seeing him when he wasn't dressed in a black suit, white shirt, and black tie. Very rarely, but on occasion, he would take off his suit coat. I often wondered if he slept in those clothes!

A vacation for my grandfather would only last for one day. He could not stand the thought that someone might die and he would not be there to help them. His whole life was the funeral business. His integrity and dedication made him one of the most highly respected members of the community. At his own death, every business in town closed during the service.

"Big Daddy" always remained a major influence in my life. I'll never forget how he always waved to everyone he met whether on the street or in the car, and he always had a kind word to say to them. I'll always remember his advice to me, "Be nice to all these people no matter what." One day I asked him "Why?" He replied, "That's the way life should be; and besides, one of these days they will die, and we want to bury them!"

After high school, I obtained a degree in mortuary science. That educational experience and training from my mentors taught me to help people deal with death through offering comforting words and through religion. In practice, they simply offered to help families through the process of planning and conducting the funeral, assuring them of caring for the details of the process. For the most part, this continues to be the only way many funeral directors support families. Aftercare has now become a way of staying in touch and giving continued support, though many times families feel it is only a means used to market them and other family members into pre-need planning for future services. I have always felt the funeral director could do more. Is there any reason to deviate from what has worked in the past? In so many ways, we know that what has worked yesterday and today won't work tomorrow. I feel it is time to look at new ways to make sense of death and funerals.

While I had always encouraged families to use poems, scriptures, and music that reflected the person's life, the services were almost always the same, conducted by a minister – who may or may not have known the deceased – delivering the same message over and over again regardless. While ministers serve an important role in the service, few things are more disappointing than for the minister or person conducting the service to say he did not know the deceased and then proceed to preach an evangelistic sermon of hellfire and damnation. Literally hundreds of services I have conducted were nearly carbon copies of one another, just a different name inserted for the deceased.

As *Ecclesiastes 3* reminds us (see p. 58-59), there is a time and place for everything. I have always thought that this was the time to reflect on a person's life – not to be preached to. I understand that some individual's wishes for the service may very well be for the minister to deliver an evangelistic sermon. In this case, I fully support the desire of the deceased and encourage the family and minister to carry out those wishes.

Roger von Oech wrote in his book, *A Whack on the Side of the Head*, "Discovery consists of looking at the same thing as everyone else and thinking something different." The first time my eyes were opened to the possibility of doing things in a different way was at a friend's funeral. This service was different. It was full of music that the deceased enjoyed during his life, as well as reflections of his beliefs and his life's story. Two of his friends told of the life that was lived –

changing the focus away from the death that occurred.

After that service, I began searching for a better way – leading families into celebrating the person's life. For some, the celebration is twofold: (1) remembering the person's contributions to the lives of others, and (2) celebrating their transformation from this physical plane into one of endless beauty and love.

I encourage you and your family to plan such a celebration, allowing the loved one's memory to live on through you. As long as you live, your loved one and their influence in your life will continue to live through you. Remember the life and freely share it with others and the death will be honored.

Bob Proctor, a leader in personal growth development, has been a great influence in my life. Bob's treasury of understanding explains why we think or don't think in the ways we do or don't – and how that affects our behavior and results in our life. Old "paradigms," habits of thinking, are programmed as we are growing up by family and peers that were programmed by their family and peers that were programmed by their family and peers and so on. These old paradigms prevent us from recognizing new and better ideas. We reject them because they do not fit into our predetermined ways of thinking.

Our old paradigms are directing what we think about death and funerals. While my grandfather and father, along with so many other funeral directors, have been loved, respected, and admired for the care they have given to the families of the deceased, they only focused on the death that occurred – not the life that was lived. Let's look at perhaps our old paradigms that were formed about death and funerals. Many people remember as a child going to a funeral or being present when their parents were preparing to go to a funeral: getting dressed up in uncomfortable clothes, tense emotions, being denied doing something fun for a few hours, having to sit still forever, the somber mood and tears, confusion, a boring person talking for a long time, being forced to see the dead person in a casket, and perhaps even being told the deceased was asleep and wondering if that would happen the next time they went to sleep. It is not a wonder we do not like funerals as adults!

Death symbolizes almost everything we are taught to deplore and fear in life. Even more resistance results from the fact that it is beyond choice or control. Little wonder then that in most cultures, death is preceded and followed by so much sadness and bereavement.

Now, let's shift our thinking to a celebration. People sharing stories, hugging each other, laughing, sharing photos, uplifting music, and even fireworks and hot dogs.

"No way, Jose! That's not like any funeral I've ever attended," you're thinking. CHANGES . . . CHOICES . . . THE FINAL CHOICE IS YOURS.

If you are feeling uncomfortable, it is because you are beginning to break out of an old paradigm. New insights from this book will allow you to have positive experiences when you are faced with the death of a loved one. I am not saying that what you may have done in the past was right or wrong. The following chapters, however, present other options for dealing with death. You can make choices for the future which coincide with your heart's desires. I know from experience there are better options than the ones we have traditionally followed.

. . .

Repeat this affirmation aloud:
"I am not too old to do new things. Life is con-
sciousness, not years. I know that I am capable
and ready to experience new and enjoyable things. I
let go of thinking I am alone or too old, because that
is not the truth. I go forward with excitement,
enthusiasm, and expectancy of all the good life has
to offer!"

. . .

Chapter 3
Why Talk About It?

Why do anything? It won't really matter. Just leave well enough alone. I don't like changes! THOUGHTS!! Those little voices in your head saying, "Do it. Don't do it." The expression is often said, "A penny for your thoughts." Well, I am going to give you a few dollars worth.

Many people say they do not want to talk about death because it will not matter – they'll be dead! "Just throw me in a pine box or cremate me; nobody cares anyway."

I beg your pardon. In all the years I have been involved in the funeral business, I have yet to have a funeral service where no one came or cared for the deceased. Such an event is extremely rare. No matter the occupation or status in the community, everyone makes a difference. Your life is important. Did you know that everyone is a leader? Of course, some are leaders in a negative way, others in a positive way. No matter what your life will be or is about, you are influencing others around you.

Scary, huh! Think about it. Your life is valuable What you choose to do with it is up to you. And, what you choose to do about your death is also up to you. Your death is valuable as well.

You might be thinking, "Now wait a minute. My *death* is valuable?" Yes. Just as it makes a difference in how a person chooses to live his or her life. At death, it makes a difference as to how we recognize that life. Why do anything? Because doing nothing also makes a difference.

People are always trying to find a way out of or around death. Unfortunately, death occurs and you are forced to deal with it. Having to make final plans for someone you love is a big task – all the choices, all the decisions. There is no right way or wrong way. "The perfect funeral is no funeral at all," some have said. To deny, however, that a life was lived is not a good answer.

Perhaps the cost of a funeral is the reason some people are reluctant to make decisions about final arrangements. Spending a lot of money is not necessary, however. Actually, after reading this book, you may find that you might save money and the decisions will be easier. For most, decisions are very difficult at the time of death and grieving.

Death is not something most people understand nor are we offered opportunities to learn about it (except the mention of Egyptians and their mummies while in school or the doctrinal teachings on heaven and hell at church). Most people refuse to talk about it in the course of their daily lives. We only deal with death when an occurrence forces us to do so.

When my first child entered elementary school, her teacher asked if her parents would be able to attend the PTA meeting. My daughter replied, "My mom will be here for sure, and my daddy will be here if nobody dies." This took the teacher by surprise. She had not met me and did not know of my occupation. Shortly thereafter, she requested a parent/teacher conference and shared her concerns about my daughter talking about people dying. Obviously, this was a problem for the teacher, not my daughter. Even with the explanation of my occupation, she thought it strange that anyone would talk about death around a child.

If talk of death is focused on the life that was

lived and a celebration of the next phase of our eternal journey, perhaps it would change the way we feel about death. Now that way of thinking would be a big change for most people. We all resist change at first. Change can, however, bring positive results into your life. For example, is your favorite music still produced on vinyl records? Of course not, tapes and CD's are a significant improvement in convenience and quality. As technology doubles at an ever rapid pace, change has become inherent in our society. In the funeral business, for example, cremation was rarely a consideration years ago. Now it is used widely across the world.

No matter who you are, at some point in your life, you will have choices and decisions to make about death. The purpose for this book is to challenge some of the old paradigms about death that were passed on to you and me by past generations.

We are a nonphysical being living in a physical body. In the book, *Born Rich*, Bob Proctor emphasizes that we live in a body – we are not a body. Look at it this way: You are "wearing" a body the same as you are wearing the clothes you have on now. It houses your mind and spirit.

There is a form of higher, far superior form of intelligence than ours. I choose to call that God. I am reminded of the story of Val Vandewall who paused for a break during one of his classes. A man walked up, apparently annoyed, and asked to speak with Mr. Vandewall concerning his references to God. Mr. Vandewall, busy at the time with another student, removed a flower from a vase and handed it to the student saying, "I'll be with you in just a moment. Would you please make another one of these while you're waiting?" Of course he couldn't; and until such time someone does, I will make reference to the Bible and God, my Higher Divine Spirit.

Whatever your belief as to the Spirit, most agree that the part of you that causes the body to see, do, be in this life . . . is absent from the body at death. I have often referred to death as like a peanut. The body is only the shell that's left. The nut is gone!

. . .

Repeat this affirmation aloud:
"All the angers, the hurts, the self-pity, and the mourning no longer hold me entrenched! I now let go of the past and live happily in the here and now!"

. . .

Do not stand by my grave and weep
I am not there, I do not sleep.
I am the thousand winds that blow.
I am the diamond glint on snow.
I am the sunlight in ripened grain.
I am the gentle autumn rain.
When you awake in the morning hush,
I am the swift uplifting rush
Of quiet birds in circling flight.
I am the soft starshine of night.
Do not stand by my grave and cry.
I am not there. I did not die.
                                        Unknown

Chapter 4
Getting Off the Rollercoaster

I had been programmed to believe that families would express their grief through crying and hysteria when told of a loved one's death and that most families would come to a "boiling point" at the initial viewing of the deceased. As a result, when I took my first family into the viewing state room to see their loved one, I was the first one to start crying because I knew what was coming. While I don't believe that it is wrong for a man to express his emotions through crying, I do know it is difficult to support others if your own emotions are out of control. This was when I first realized I had to change me before I could help others.

At that time, I realized that we all need to learn how to handle our emotions or else we are in for a roller-coaster ride of ups and downs – highs and lows – that depletes our energy, our health, and our personal relationships with those around us. The way we deal with our emotions is learned, for the most part, while we are growing up. Many adults, however, never achieve emotional maturity. Even individuals of high intelligence with responsible positions are unable to deal with their emotions during the death of a family member or close friend.

When death occurs, we often find ourselves being ruled by our emotions. Unfortunately, when we hang on to negative emotions over an extended period of time, physical effects begin to surface. *Anger*, for instance, is an emotion that people experience through grief which closes down their metabolism and their stress level increases dramatically. This can cause a range of illnesses from simple headaches to even their own death.

A very common emotion experienced by many is *guilt*. Guilt is very difficult to handle. Most of us are forever trying to gain approval from others. If approval is not given or is taken away, we feel guilty and let ourselves be manipulated into the most insidious form of guilt – which is self-imposed. Self-inflicted guilt is a neurotic type of behavior. It is impossible to change the past. We have all done things that we wish we could change, and we all make mistakes at times. It is natural. It is not natural, however, to spend the rest of our lives punishing ourselves for our past failings. Too often, individuals get stuck in the negative and pointless rut of wondering, "What if . . . ."

Bitterness brings on a strong surge of emotions. "I can't believe he did this to me," the widow exclaimed with despair. "How could he? House payments, kids to raise – what am I going to do? It's a good thing he's dead or I'd kill him!" Because of bitterness, some funeral services not only show disregard to the life of the deceased but compounds the difficulty of survivors to handle the situation.

Disbelief is one of the toughest emotions. When the police come to the door and announce a loved one's death in an accident, the first response is disbelief, confusion, numbness. "Are you sure it was him? Couldn't there be a mistake? Mistakes have happened before."

I know individuals who have never accepted the fact that death occurred to their loved one. All the evidence shows it was their loved one, but they still choose to disbelieve. Refusing to face the fact of death is only a means of escape by pretending that death did not occur. This only compounds the problem, for to delay acceptance is to multiply grief.

Someone once told me that I would probably see a family at the funeral home approximately every ten years due to deaths that would occur in a family. I do not think, however, that person knew the impact of an emotion we tend to forget – *loneliness*. Loneliness is an emotional killer. So many people have said to me, "We just buried our mom last year. Dad never was the same after that." Why? Loneliness. Like all the other emotions, however, we each make our own choices as to how we deal with it.

Let's just tell it like it is – anger, guilt, bitterness, disbelief, loneliness, heartache, anxiety, fear, and denial are emotions most often felt when death occurs. All of these emotions have a profound effect on our lives. They are negative emotions that we do not like to deal with. So naturally, we try to avoid the subject of death. Remember, however, to deliberately make the choice to focus on the positive – no matter the situation. We can choose how we handle our emotions. How? If we need help in moving to positive feelings, sometimes it can be more quickly realized by making a change (even for just a few hours or days) to a different environment, different people whom we are around, or feeding our mind and soul with positive reading material.

In 1969, the concept of "stages" was popularized with the publication of Elizabeth Kubler-Ross's book, "On Death and Dying." Kubler-Ross identifies five psychological stages or coping mechanisms of dying or reactions to one's awareness of imminent death: (1) denial and isolation ("No, not me; it can't be true!"); (2) anger-rage, envy, resentment ("Why me?"); (3) bargaining ("If you'll . . . then I'll . . ."); (4) depression ("What's the use?"); and (5) acceptance (the final rest before the long journey). According to her analysis, "the one thing that persists through all these stages is hope ("I will not die.").

Thinking of death in a stage-like process may be appealing to a lot of people and may have actually helped some individuals make sense out of death. These attempts, however, only allow us to mask our fear and lack of understanding by saying we are "going through a stage."

We have to come to the complete understanding that each person's emotions are uniquely his or her own. I think we only get in trouble when we tell someone what they should be feeling. I have often heard people say to a grieving individual, "Just get over it. Get a hold of yourself. Stop crying; it's not going to help. You're upsetting everyone else." Then the person will respond, "I can't help it," or "You don't understand."

Refusing to allow tears, suffering in silence, and "being strong," are thought by some to be admirable behaviors. The results of this kind of avoidance of emotions can be even more harmful. Be true to yourself. Do not let others influence your emotions.

We cannot control death. We can, however, recognize our emotions and control the way we react to them when they surface. Admittedly, saying, "Pick up your life and move on," is easier said than done. It is important for you to take whatever amount of time you need to deal with a loved one's death. Do not be misled to think, however, that time alone will heal your loss. Thomas D. Willhite wrote, "If you don't like the way you feel, change it. It is your responsibility." Unfortunately, we often refuse to change because we think that to change is to admit we were wrong in the first place.

It is not easy to take charge of our emotions. Although we do not want to admit it, sometimes we do not want to take control of our emotions and our life because we are getting some benefit or satisfaction from continuing in our current behavior. Be certain, however, that it is important for you to accept the responsibility that you and you alone can handle your emotions. The fact is, your emotions are your responsibility; and if they are going to change, it is totally up to you. Do you choose to celebrate the life that was lived and let that memory live on through you or are you going to make the choice to suffer in your negative state of mind?

We all face conflicts and difficulties in our lives How we deal with our emotions during these situations is of the utmost importance. Unless we deal with them constructively, they will continue to interfere with our lives either on a conscious or subconscious level. Our emotions demand expression and an action from us.

So, how do we change? To help us deal with our emotions and focus on changing to a new attitude about death, we can seek help through prayer. The power of prayer can create shifts in your emotions. Be mindful of your thoughts, living in and praying in a state of peace, harmony, and love as often as you can.

So many people do not know how to pray. In prayer, we are calling upon a higher intelligence who has the power to support or change whatever we desire. In calling on God, for example, you are summoning in a very powerful way, your own qualities of love, compassion, forgiveness, and healing ability.

Amazing results happen through prayer. To truly pray, we not only summon the essence of a higher intelligence and being, we ask of our subconscious to give of ourselves. Many amazing changes and results of prayer are achieved by simply making a strong, clear statement to yourself that you are receiving the energy you want or need.

Try praying in a comfortable position and place – alone. Relax . . . close your eyes . . . think of a pleasant place . . . visualize it, see yourself a part of it. Take deep breaths. Imagine something good, pleasant, enjoy being a part of this experience. Now call upon God. Thank God for being with you. Express your desires. Thank Him for loving you and giving you your highest divine good. Know you are receiving it.

Dear Father Mother God, my Higher Power,
Please open my eyes so I may understand.
I pray for your wisdom;
I pray for your guidance;
I thank you for your protection and all your good.
                                                                Blanche Lukes

Mark 11:24 tells us, "Therefore I tell you, whatever you ask for in prayer, believe that you have received it, and it will be yours."

Most people underestimate and do not realize the power of their thoughts. Actually, our life is what we have thought about. Thoughts are things. Radio waves exist even though we cannot see them. In the same way, brainwaves exist. You can measure them with an electroencephalogram (EEG). They affect you and the world around you more profoundly than you probably realize.

You can feel the power of your thoughts by observing your feelings and your body when you are thinking fearful, negative thoughts versus loving, positive ones. Try it now by taking a few moments to remember the death of a loved one or a time you were very angry. Your body will begin to feel the same way it did then.

I am reminded of a time when I was a child, seeing a dog in the highway as a car was approaching. I attempted to get the dog to run off the road, but to no avail. Witnessing the dog being hit by the car was a terrible experience. My emotions raged with anger toward the driver for hitting the dog; anger toward the dog for not coming to me when I called. I was overwhelmed with sadness and pain, seeing the dog rolled under the car. My body cringes even now from remembering the experience. It reacts now much as the same then.

Now concentrate on a beautiful experience you had with your children, spouse, or friend. You'll feel better right away. Maybe you remember the first time your child, in diapers and perhaps barefooted, let go of the coffee table and walked across the room to your open arms, smiling from ear to ear. Do you already feel a sense of warmth, relaxation, and maybe some tingling with happiness and excitement?

The sooner you understand the power of positive thoughts and take action to make this shift, the sooner healing can take place. This healing benefits not only you, but also everyone around you.

Life events and death do not have any meaning except the meaning we give to them. The application of the meaning of death becomes your own reality. Dr. John Mike, psychiatrist and author of *Brilliant Babies, Powerful Adults*, writes, "When I treat patients who believe that they see the reality of how things are in their relationships or in their lives, I tell them, 'There are over five billion people in this world, and there are over five billion realities.'"

Look at the drawing on page 42. What do you see? You would perhaps describe the woman as about 25 to 35 years old, attractive, fashionable, and maybe

sophisticated.

Now turn to page 44 and look at the picture and describe what you see. Do you see a young woman again, much like the one on page 42?

What would you say if I told you that the drawing on page 44 is a woman between 60 to 80 years old, has a huge nose, and looks rather sad? You might say, "No way. She is in her 30's, at the most, and beautiful." We could go on arguing, each supporting and arguing the "facts."

Now look at the third drawing on page 46 of the older woman. Go back then to the second drawing on page 44. Do you now see the older woman as well as the young woman. This is a clear example of how we "pre-frame" the world through our own little box or programmed minds. Then we call it "reality."

Basically, the way we handle our emotions and change the death of a loved one into a more positive experience is by controlling our thoughts and changing our reality. We essentially create our reality. When an emotion surfaces, we have a choice as to what to do with it. We need to take charge of the most powerful influences in our lives, our emotions.

Past experiences and the uncertainties about death have caused negative paradigms for most of us. The great news is that we can remove these paradigms that hold us back from dealing with death in a positive way. When you think and focus on negative emotions, that is where you will remain. When you focus on positive emotions, a peaceful calm, loving emotional state will take place. It really is your choice.

I am reminded of a woman who I had counseled prior to a funeral service. She had a great understand-

ing of death but was confused because she did not feel the deep depression and sadness she thought she should. Her positive emotions were a result of focusing on the life she had shared with the deceased. The confusion came from implications of her friends and family that she should be hysterical and upset. The prevailing gossip centered around questions of her love and devotion for her now deceased mother.

I advised her to not worry about the others and their expectations. Then I shared a story about my mother (Philosophy According to Mama Fay). My mother never had a separate living room and den or family room in our home because she always said, "If guests at our home can't sit where I sit everyday, then they shouldn't be here." Essentially, she did not care what other people thought and was not going to get into the game of competing with the "Joneses."

As the woman walked by the casket for the final time, I was shocked when she broke down, cried hysterically and grabbed onto the casket. She had to be helped to her car. As I approached her sitting in the car she winked at me with a smile and said, "I, unfortunately, have a living room and a den. That 'little show' was for the others. I'm still doing O.K."

The games we play – the rollercoaster we ride through life for the satisfaction of others and ourselves! Are you ready to get off of the rollercoaster?

Emotions are as much a part of our lives as breathing. We can not live life to its fullest without them. To hold back our emotions and the expression of them is not the answer to a happy, fulfilled life. We must focus toward positive thoughts and release or let go of our negative thoughts. Replace and cleanse negative emotions with pleasant, pleasing thoughts. You can make grief good; but it will only happen if you change your focus. The only limitations you have in doing so are the ones you put on your-

self. Having good grief does make more sense.

"We do not have to lose heart. While outwardly we are wasting away, yet inwardly we are being renewed day by day. For our light and momentary troubles are achieving for us an eternal glory that far outweighs them all. We should fix our eyes not on what is seen, but what is unseen. For what is seen is temporary, but what is unseen is eternal" 2 Corinthians 4:16-18 (NIV).

. . .

Repeat this affirmation aloud:
"I now no longer react. I stop, breathe and simply respond in a positive, loving, non-attached way, which in turn heals my soul!"

"I now appreciate all that life has to offer. I now let go of the past to enjoy a new plane of peace and love!"

"This is my life. I make a difference! Oh, how I love my new life, here and now!"

Chapter 5
Your Eternal Journey

Unlike a clear blue sky in which we can seemingly see forever, our lives are sometimes like a storm. Clouds roll in and obscure our view. Life is like that. Just when we are happy or content with ourselves and our surroundings, clouds roll in. At times they are small and quickly pass on. When death occurs, however, large unending storm clouds cover our life and the rain begins.

Like the sky, circumstances in our lives change. Our hope for a happy future seemingly is covered or taken away. All we dreamed of doing and having with the loved one, now dead, has been destroyed. Storms come and go. So do our loved ones. We, however, do have a choice: remain in the dark, resisting the option of leaving the storm or go beyond the clouds to seek more sunshine in our lives.

"But I don't understand how this is possible," you might be thinking. Have you ever taken a trip in a plane and passed through storm clouds? Or maybe it was raining when you took off. Do you remember climbing through the storm clouds to clear and sunny skies? That's the same amazing sensation one receives when getting beyond what seems to be a negative situation.

When the clouds roll in,
the rain begins.
The wind will blow – but still we know
the sun shines bright just out of our sight.
Remember my friend,
the storm can end.
For what we see is what we will be.
If it is to be, it's up to me!

Death and future – what do we know about their relationship? Is there life after death? The only way we will know will be from our own experience. Some believe that salvation is the work of God whereby He delivers His people from bondage to all evil power. Viewed negatively, God's deliverance is rescue from such evils as selfish and corrupt rulers, murder and violence, injustices, death, the grave, and hell. Viewed positively, His deliverance is into life, light, love, wholeness, safety, peace, joy, freedom, and heaven. Jesus, God's Son, promised while here on earth, "Do not let your hearts be troubled. Trust in God; trust also in me. In my father's house are many rooms; if it were not so, I would have told you. I am going there to prepare a place for you" John 14:1-2 (NIV).

Many people have had what is referred to as *near death experiences.* From conversations with several of those, I have concluded that the fearful storm of death is actually the calm, blue sky beyond. Here is one such story told to me.

Drowned

"The spring sunshine brought an end to the snow that had lasted all winter," Bill shared. "The once frozen river, now flowing faster and close to its peak, had always been an invitation for me to come and conquer it. Weeks of planning were at an end as the six of us took to our raft. A white water adventure awaited.

" 'A thrill a minute!' one exclaimed. Then suddenly Bill was thrown out of the raft. Of course the life vest would keep him safe.

"I remember seeing the others in the raft reaching for me. I tried to grab their hands, but the current was too swift and the rapids had become violent. I was being tossed from one boulder to another. Gasping for air, I was pulled under by the strong undertow of the current for what seemed a long time.

"Where was I? What was happening? Suddenly I realized I was not struggling anymore. I was in a white light that was bright but gentle. There below me were my friends in the raft, appearing to be screaming and struggling to reach for something, but what? As I looked closer . . . I saw what appeared to be someone. It was me. I was being thrown against the rocks and pulled under the water only to be thrust back to the surface again and again . . . . Now face down in the calmer water floated the lifeless body I had observed.

"I didn't understand. I was feeling peace and joy not suffering and pain. That couldn't be me. One of my friends had jumped in the water, grasped my life vest by the collar, and pulled the limp body toward the bank of the river. Something tugged at me as I turned back toward the light. All I could think of was the desire to go toward this indescribable, beautiful light. I felt the light and felt as if I was being called to go. It was so pleasant and peaceful . . . screaming! . . .where? I looked back at the river bank. My friends, they're upset. What do I do? Can I choose?

"As I looked around the room, a nurse said, 'Welcome back; I'll get your doctor.' The doctor said I had been in a coma for several days.

"It had only seemed minutes since I was at the river. My body was bruised, and I had two broken bones. Pain and discomfort! But back in the body I had always known to be mine.

"I believe I was actually close to death or dead when this accident occurred. Whether the choice to return was mine or not, I do not know. My friends thought I was a 'goner'! The struggle they had witnessed by life being overcome by death was unforgettable. 'Boy, that was close,' they exclaimed.

"Close? Why did I come back from that peaceful light? I don't think it was a near death experience. I think I touched the face of death but only for a brief period. I do know there is calm after a storm. I now accept my life as the awaiting of the great white light with the glow all around me, covering me with the feeling of peace, love, joy – no pain or agony."

Maybe you know someone like Bill. Several books have been written about such experiences and each of them share similar stories. In Jean Ritchie's book, *Death's Door*, she explains that some have seen a light at the end of a tunnel; others have seen angels or deceased loved ones. Some have felt pain; while others felt an overwhelming joy. One common thread, however, in everyone's near death experience is that the experience changed their lives forever.

The following letter, from *Second Helping of Chicken Soup for the Soul*, was written by a 12-year-old boy to his friend Shannon before she died:

Go to the light, Shannon, where those who have gone before you wait, with anticipation of feeling your presence. They will welcome you with open arms, combined with love, laughter and feelings that are the happiest that could be possibly felt by anyone, on earth or in heaven. Shannon, there is no pain or suffering. Sadness is an absolute impossibility. When you enter the light you can play with all of your friends that mysteriously disappeared while you were so gallantly battling the evil plague of cancer, and dodging cleverly the Grim Reaper's angry hand of the darkness that he possesses.

Those that are still on earth will certainly miss you deeply and long for your sense of specialness, but you will live in their hearts and spirits. You are the reason that all people who knew you were somehow brought closer to each other. . . .

The hearts you've touched will never lose the feeling of love. So, Shannon, when you suddenly find yourself alone in a dark tunnel and a pinpoint of light is visible . . . find the courage to go into the light.

Perhaps you recall a television commercial in which a man who was killed in a car accident was escorted through the clouds by two others (who apparently were angels). The man looked at the two and said something like, "Whew, that was close. That car almost hit me!"

Their reply was "It did."

I tend to believe that death is much like this. Unlike the pain and suffering that we think must accompany death, I believe death is a peaceful transition to another life. The higher spirit that operated in our body has left for a life we can not begin to imagine. . . the next phase of our *eternal journey.*

While many prefer not to talk about death, it is a part of our future. Unlike birth, we are given the opportunity to take control over a major part of it – our service arrangements. The celebration of your life can be pre-planned. Do not be one of those who looks back and says, "If I knew then what I know now, I would have done things differently or if I could do things over again . . . ."

I have never had a family of a deceased who had pre-planned come to me and say they wish their loved one had not done so. On the other hand, I have had countless families make final plans for the deceased and ask, "Why do I have to make these decisions? I wish I knew what they would have wanted."

Each of our lives is a picture for all to see of how we have chosen to live – and to die. Taking the responsibility of pre-planning, the final gift to your loved ones, probably generates resistance on your part. Maybe you have already been the victim of telemarketing programs trying to persuade you to prearrange your services at a particular funeral home. If not, more than likely you will receive a call in the future. Pre-planning of your last arrangements may be something you have not thought about, but it deserves your consideration.

After reading the chapter, "Choosing a Funeral Director," you will see that making decisions over the phone is not recommended. While many funeral homes have excellent plans from which you can choose, you should decide first what you want from a funeral director and the type of services you desire.

What does pre-planning mean? Pre-planning is an opportunity to consider and determine the arrangements and events to take place upon the occurrence of death. It is a final gift you can give to your loved ones. Leaving your family with all the decisions of planning a service can be an overwhelming burden. Pre-planning is a final choice and a gift. Each of our lives is a picture for all to see of how we have chosen to live – and to die. Furthermore, pre-planning can, and in most cases will, save you and your family money.

Why would a person not pre-plan? The number one reason is that most people do not want to talk about death – especially their own. Let's get real. This old paradigm must go. We are all going to die. To leave your loved ones with no pre-planned arrangements is much like that gift you opened one time that was nothing that you would ever want or use and you wondered what you would do with it!

Some think that Social Security or Veteran's death benefits will take care of them. You need to understand, however, that changes have been made in these programs which have limited the benefits to the extent that they do not, in most cases, cover the costs of a typical burial or cremation. Leaving a financial burden coupled with the emotional burden of making the decisions is likely not the way you want to leave your family.

Do not feel as though you need to plan every detail of your arrangements. Some will want to be very detailed; others will simply leave general guidance as to how they want things done. If you have ever had a party or a little "get together" for friends or family, you know that without planning the event properly it will not be a good or optimum experience for everyone.

As time goes on, you can always add or change ideas. After all, what you want now could change – oh, yea, I know you do not want anything now, but play along with me. Read the chapter, "My Example." For the most part, this is the celebration I want at the event of my own death. Although it may change as my life evolves, this plan is my final gift to my loved ones.

A lady, now deceased, came to me to make her final plans. After some time, she decided exactly what she wanted for her services. Her hardest decision was choosing the casket. She could not decide which one she would "look the best in."

To make a long story short, she had a photograph taken in the clothes she would be buried in and placed it in the casket she had chosen so she could see how she would look!

. . .

Repeat this affirmation aloud:
"I now expand into a greater idea for myself. I now expand into a universe of inner growth, understanding, and truth!"

. . .

Chapter 6
The New Concept

The time that we have here on earth is a gift from God. "I know that there is nothing better for men than to be happy and do good while they live. That everyone may eat and drink, and find satisfaction in all his toil – this is the gift of God." Ecclesiastes 3:12-13 (NIV).

To focus on what we will not have as a result of death is of no value. *You are about to enter a whole new concept about death.* Be open minded, read this several times. Be willing to open your mind and consider new thoughts. It can make a *huge* difference in how you look at life as well as death.

Several basic decisions have to be made when death occurs. What I want you to focus on now is our view, attitude, or perspective of death. Death is not negative, unless you make it negative. We have a choice.

The intent is not to try to get you to forget your loved one. Rather, it is to enhance your thoughts and memories of the life and love you shared. By the way, life should not be measured by the number of years we live but by the contributions we made to others. Whether you realize it or not, each of us makes contributions to others every day – they are either negative or positive contributions to the people we come in contact with.

One man really struggled with the death of his wife. He said, "We did everything together. I can't go on without her. It's too sad. I think of her no matter what I do." Even though this man was young, he felt his life was destroyed. He "buried" himself with her. Perhaps you have known of similar situations.

When someone you love dies, no matter how prepared you try to be, you will usually be somewhat surprised, confused, and emotionally distraught. That is normal. Questions about how or why they died when they did and the overwhelming emotions revolving around death can push you to feel like your life has been turned upside down. It is O.K. to have these feelings, and you will need some time to deal with them. You are grieving. Remember, however, that time alone will not heal nor can it heal. For you to remain in a negative state is not healthy or for your highest good. Remember, it is up to you to control your thoughts which in turn control your emotions.

When death occurs, many people are never quite satisfied with the reason it happened to the one they loved. Of course, they have the doctor's or coroner's report, but that never seems complete or thorough enough. After all, we have heard the stories about how others have survived a similar incident or were cured of a similar disease. Most continue to wonder what the doctors or someone else might have done wrong. Many wonder why they were not granted a last-minute healing.

Well, it is *choice* time. Either stay in these thoughts or move on. Continue to think in the ways we have been programmed, which is the easiest thing to do, or **make death a positive experience**. You have the choice of looking at the positive side of death. Make death a celebration not only of the life that was lived but also their passing into the next phase of their eternal adventure.

There is a time for everything,
and a season for every activity under heaven:
a time to be born and a time to die,
a time to plant and a time to uproot,
a time to kill and a time to heal,
a time to tear down and a time to build,

a time to weep and a time to laugh,
a time to mourn and a time to dance,
a time to scatter stones and a time to gather them,
a time to embrace and a time to refrain,
a time to search and a time to give up,
a time to keep and a time to throw away,
a time to tear and a time to mend,
a time to be silent and a time to speak,
a time to love and a time to hate,
a time for war and a time for peace.

Ecclesiastes 3:2-8 (NIV)

So, will you be stuck in a time slot, such as "a time to mourn?" How long will you stay there? When will it be a time to dance? The decision is yours. It has been said, "Life demands that man must confront situations – sometimes to change the situation, other times to change himself."

Everything in the universe has an opposite. Realize that every situation JUST IS, you make it negative or positive by virtue of how you choose to think about the situation. When you look at the situation one way, it appears to be negative. You can change your perspective and look at it from the opposite viewpoint, it will be positive. You have the power to choose which side you will take.

In our subconscious mind, we store mental pictures or images. Now, imagine for a moment a beautiful sunset across the ocean. Listen to the gentle waves as they roll in. Feel the sand move around your feet. Feel the warm breeze blow against your body. Take a deep breath of fresh air. Close your eyes and imagine yourself standing there.

Pleasant thoughts such as these will relax our body. When we focus on an idea in our mind, our body reacts accordingly. If we focus on a negative idea which brings horrible images to our mind, it affects how we feel almost instantly.

When we think about death, what kind of images do we have. How does it make us feel? Most people have negative images and thoughts which they cling to and justify based on their past experiences. But where would you prefer to be? If negative images move you into a negative feeling or vibration and happy images move you into a good feeling or positive vibration, choose happy thoughts and feel good!

When death occurs, our mind tends to go in this direction: "I can't live without him." "I should have done something." "I wish I'd . . . ." "How will I ever make ends meet?" Just saying these things gives you a bad feeling. Picture a mother bending over her son's body in the casket screaming and crying uncontrollably. How does this image feel? I know, most readers do not need my help coming up with negative images about death.

In the past, I felt it was best to help a family by focusing on the death, thinking that it would help them accept the death and move on with their life. (A person has to accept the death before he or she can deal with grief, so I had been taught.) For example, when a family would come to me to make arrangements, I would ask questions such as the following: "How long has he been sick?" "When did you notice something was wrong?" "Had the deceased been to a doctor recently?" "How much weight did he or she lose?" Then I would reply, "Well, at least he (or she) won't have to suffer anymore." If the death was a result of an accident, I would ask questions pertaining to the circumstances. I realize now that this line of questioning and thinking was keeping them focused on negative images.

So, where is the positive side? How can we move in that direction? For me as a funeral director, my focus when meeting with a family after death occurs is entirely different. My questions now relate to the life prior to the deceased illness or cause of death. By doing so, the family begins focusing on meaningful moments they shared. Sometimes this will bring tears but more often not.

Of course, I cannot assure you that other funeral directors will use this approach. My purpose for sharing this with you, however, is so that you can use this in your own experience when around others who have had loved ones die.

I have heard my wife talk about "ah-hah moments" when attending seminars or other opportunities for learning. "Ah-hah moments" happen when you learn something new that really "turns you on," or you suddenly see something old in a new or different way that excites you. The rest of this chapter shares some ideas that may be "ah-hah" moments for you.

Ah-hah #1
Moments. The key to the new concept of celebrating the life that was lived is meaningful moments. Each of us has meaningful moments. They can be simple, spontaneous, or planned events in our lives. Examples of moments to remember include the following: How you met the person, a trip or vacation you shared, children's births, a special party, the wedding, a simple conversation, a joke shared, and so on.

My 10-year old daughter creates meaningful moments for me with her creative writing. She has written a book of poems called "Just Stuff" which she shares with me on occasion. One of the poems I especially enjoyed her sharing is as follows:

To Keep You Happy . . .
Life is life
and life is life
You want anymore
You read it again!

You may think that some moments will be personal and special only to you; but when shared with others, they will feel the positive emotions you do. I can not help but grin and have good vibrations all over when I share Lauren's poetry thoughts! Can you feel that just reading this?

Moments are what the person's life was all about. Everyone has moments that are special with the people they know and love. By friends and family sharing those moments during the service, everyone's focus will be lifted toward the life that was lived and their contribution to the lives they touched.

Ah-hah #2

Need help remembering special moments? Ah-hah! Pull out the photo albums and home movies. So often they are on the shelf covered with dust. Now is the time to get them out as family and friends gather. Fill the table or floor with photos. Choose several favorites and make a "memory board" of the person's life. (Some funeral homes provide a display board especially for this use.) Include family and friends in the pictures. You may want to enlarge selected photos for display at particular areas where you are having the service or gathering afterwards. Remember, a picture is worth a thousand words.

Ah-hah #3

Visually depict a person's life at their memorial celebration. Display items at the service that were a part of or represent the life of the deceased. Each person has hobbies or special interests during their lifetime. They may have been outdoor activities: skiing, hunting, fishing, hiking, running, diving, photography, horseback riding, golf, gardening. The list is endless. What about indoor activities? Painting, canning, sewing, reading, writing, music. Did the person support a favorite sports team either locally or professional? Did he or she wear a special hat or cap? Do you get the idea?

Now, gather items that represent that person's life. Have them displayed at the service.

Ah-hah #4

Music! What are some songs that reflect the essence of that person's life? What music and artists did they enjoy? Play the music; and while listening, select some songs you would like played before or during the service. Sure you can play rock 'n' roll, country, or jazz. You do not have to be limited by traditional religious music. Do not worry about what everyone will think. I often tell families that if someone does not like or approve of something, "Blame it on me – you have enough on your mind." I remember the Black services I attended in Tennessee would be filled with upbeat music that would find me tapping my foot or swaying with the beat. There is nothing wrong with upbeat music.

Ah-hah #5

Eat, drink, and be merry! Do not drink to forget; but celebrate with food and drink. Continue sharing moments with a "fellowship period" after the service. This could be at someone's home, a restaurant, or in the fellowship hall at the church. The service will remind others of meaningful moments they had that they will share during the fellowship period. Display photos for everyone's enjoyment and remembrance.

Ah-hah #6

"I like hugs and I like kisses, but what I like most is help with the dishes!" You do not have to do everything for yourself by yourself to prove anything. Your family and friends will want to help you in anyway you ask. Use them; you are not abusing them by doing so. Maybe you just need a hug or kiss; but believe me, there are still the dishes! The key to a full life is sharing the whole pie. Slap some ice cream on it too!

The following describes what I feel to be the optimum service arrangements for putting everything together. The service is a celebration in a "memorial service" format. Most of it can be adapted for a traditional service where the body/casket is present. If the body is present, I recommend closing the casket prior to the service and never opening it again. Any viewing should take place prior to time for the service. Furthermore, I prefer the burial prior to the memorial celebration service. This is probably a real paradigm shift for most, but give it some thought. Reversing the traditional order of doing things enhances the flow of the memorial celebration, pushing the course of events toward an ever increasing positive feeling. No matter how you do it, the last thing people should see when leaving a service is the memories of the life lived not the body of the deceased.

In preparation for the public service, take the memory photo board you have prepared and place it where people enter for the service. A good place would be wherever the register book is placed. This gives everyone coming to the service an immediate focus on the life that was lived. It will also spark pleasant memories they, too, have of your loved one.

In the front of the room, where the casket would normally be, place a table (card table with a cloth works fine) and various flower stands. Display the items you have brought, including photos, on the stands and table. You might put a photo of an outdoor activity on a stand with items from that activity sitting around it. For example, a photo of golfing would have the golf bag or some favorite clubs nearby. Accent and complete the background with plants and flowers that may have been sent for the service.

The stage is set! Of course, your funeral director can assist you with the set up and arrangement of items and flowers. This is when you may ask a friend to assist you so you do not have to be responsible. Play the music you have selected before the service as people arrive as well as during the service. Meaningful moments now bring everything together for the celebration. The person officiating will make appropriate comments, then have some friends and/or family members prepared to share some of their moments spent with the deceased.

You may also choose to allow time to open the service for anyone present who wishes to share spontaneously additional feelings or memories. I would advise you to do this with caution, however. Sometimes people go on and on; and before you know it, the service is twice as long as you ever imagined. You have to decide if that is O.K. for you. I must warn you also that you should be prepared for the spontaneity of the situation, depending on the people in attendance.

To explain, here is a true story from a service I conducted. During the time for sharing moments, a friend of the deceased relayed the story of how "Billy Bob and me had some great times fishing. One time he caught this huge trout, and it took him forever to get it landed. He fell down twice, and I did once getting over to help him. We were soaked to the bone, laughing and spinning around trying not to get tangled in the line. When he got the hook out of the fish, he rubbed its belly and let it go! Man, that was a pretty fish. He said he'd rather try and catch it again someday or let someone else have the fun instead of putting it on his wall to brag about. Yep, we sat on the bank of the river and smoked us a big ole joint after that . . . he always had some great pot!"

I am not sharing this experience because I am a proponent of drugs or approve of what this man shared at the service. I use it as an illustration to help you realize that sometimes the sharing may be funny, shocking, or sad . . . but you will see people perhaps more open and honest than at any other time in their lives. When we reminisce, it can serve as a healing for all concerned.

Our life becomes an open book, and it is read at this service. More often than not, I have seen friends and family leave this type of service smiling and nodding their heads at one another with pleasant memories instead of bent double in grief.

After the service, go to the place you have chosen for the fellowship time. You may wish to allow time between to go home and change clothes. Be sure to take some of the photos, memory board, flowers, or other items with you.

Keep asking yourself, "Where is my focus?" Choose to think of the loss you suffer from that person's death or choose to remember the special moments or gifts that person contributed to your life.

Depending on your beliefs about life after death, your focus can be stronger with even more reason to celebrate. As many of us believe, this life on earth is only one phase of our eternal journey. The gentle push we receive into the next phase is an event to look forward to. It is with great anticipation that some of us expect to live a far superior existence and experience with God in the rest of our eternal journey. If this is your belief, by all means celebrate the passing of your loved one into the next life! Your celebrations should be the biggest of them all!

When we are overwhelmed by the circumstances around us, it is difficult to do what we know to do or want to do. Controlling our thoughts and emotions is not easy! To shift our thinking may require some understanding of how the conscious and subconscious mind work. Read the next paragraphs closely, because the facts you learn here can impact all areas of your life immediately.

To bring order and understanding to your mind, you must have an image to work with. Since your mind is the unseen part of your personality, you must engage your imagination to build this image. Bob Proctor, whom I mentioned earlier, uses the stickperson to help us understand the mind.

The stickperson is extremely simple. Do not allow the apparent simplicity to deceive you, for the stickperson concept can reveal to you a wonderful world of power, possibility and promise.

You have a power within you (God, Spirit) that is far superior to any condition or circumstance around you. With *free will*, your thoughts direct this power to whatever results you choose. The conscious mind, the part of you that thinks, reasons, is where the *free will* lies.

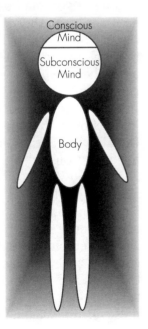

The conscious mind can accept or reject any idea. No person or circumstance can cause you to think about thoughts or ideas you do not choose. The "thoughts" you choose eventually determine the results in your life. All pain, pleasure, or limitation is either originated in the conscious mind, or accepted uncritically from an outside source. The conscious portion of the mind has the power of choice. As you choose or accept a thought, it is impressed upon the second part of your personality – the subconscious mind.

The subconscious mind is the most magnificent part of you; it is the power center. It functions in every cell of your body. Every thought your conscious mind chooses to accept, this part *must* accept . . . it has no ability to reject it.

The subconscious part of you operates in an orderly manner. It expresses itself through you in feelings and actions. Any thought you consciously choose to impress upon the subconscious over and over becomes fixed in this part of your personality. Fixed ideas will then continue to express themselves without any conscious assistance, until they are replaced. (Fixed ideas are more commonly referred to as habits.) The subconscious mind is the portion of you that is Spirit, connected to God. It knows no limits, save those you consciously choose.

Your body is the most obvious part of you, the material medium. It is merely an instrument of the mind, or the house you live in. The thoughts or images that are consciously chosen, impressed upon the subconscious (which is in every cell of your body), must move your body into action. Those actions then determine your results. Get all three of these parts working in harmony in a positive vibration and your true potential can be realized.

Know that when your conscious mind begins accepting thoughts that are different from your old paradigms or ways of thinking that are lodged in your subconscious mind, you will feel very uncomfortable. You will be tempted to step back into safety, back into your comfort zone. Proceed and step forward with the new thoughts and the uncomfortable feeling will leave as the subconscious (old conditioning) changes. When you feel these uncomfortable feelings, "You will either step forward into growth, or you will step back into safety." (Abraham Maslow)

To help you with this process, read the following affirmations aloud. Feed these thoughts consciously to your subconscious mind. Begin changing the old conditioning and feel good about this positive change in your perception of life and death!

. . .

Repeat this affirmation aloud:
"I now remember all the beautiful experiences I had with my loved one, and I now am filled with only the good we had together. All else disappears as the tide disappears sand on the beach. This fills me with joy, gratitude, and self-acceptance. Now, I go forward on my own crusade of life's experience and beauty!"

. . .

Chapter 7
Special Help for Terminal Illness, Suicide, and Death of a Child

Someone once said, "I want to die peacefully in my sleep like my grandfather . . . not screaming and hollering like the other people who were riding in the car with him!"

The ways in which we die varies vastly and uniquely. The book, *How We Die*, by Serwin B. Nuland, describes the mechanisms of cancer, heart attack, stroke, aids, and Alzheimer's disease with clinical exactness but still offering sensitivity to the subject of death. Regardless of the circumstances, die we must – whether of disease, injury, infirmity, or suicide. The only unanswered questions are when and how.

Throughout my years as a funeral director, I have perhaps received the most questions and concerns about dealing with terminal illness, death of a child, and suicide. This chapter shares my thoughts regarding those circumstances of death.

First of all, there is a natural law of polarity which can be ignored but nevertheless cannot be denied. This natural law simply states that everything has an opposite: hot/cold, up/down, in/out. There would be no inside to a room without an outside. If you referred to the side of this sheet of paper as the front, then the other side would be the back. You have a left and right side of your body, a front and back.

The law not only states that everything has an opposite . . . it is equal and opposite. If it is three feet from the floor up to the table, it would be three feet from the table down to the floor. If it is 150 miles from Manchester to London, by law it must be 150 miles from London to Manchester; it could not be any other way.

If something you consider bad happens in your life, there has to be something good about it. Remember that every situation *just is*, you make it negative or positive by virtue of how you choose to think about it. When you look at the situation one way, it is negative. But when you change your perspective and look at it from the opposite viewpoint, it will be positive. The viewpoint we take is our choice.

Most of us were programmed to look at the negative. For example, in school we received our work back from the teacher with a red "X" accenting the wrong answers and our failures. How different might we have felt if the paper came back with perhaps a "green" check beside every *correct* answer?

To further prove this point to yourself, ask someone to watch as you begin writing addition facts on a piece of paper: 4+4=8, 10+10=20, 9+9=15, 7+7=14. If they do not call your attention to 9+9=15 as soon as you write it as being wrong, give them a few more moments – they will!

Notice, they did not say you have three correct. When you read the figures, did you think it was a misprint? How easily and quickly we call attention to the negative. We are not programmed to acknowledge the correct answers – on the contrary, we look for imperfections – what is going wrong rather than what is going right.

. . .

Read this affirmation aloud:
"I am now so filled with the divine melody of life that all veils of sorrow are now replaced with inner love and peace!"

. . .

Terminal Illness

Life for the terminally ill person tends to focus on, cling to, and dwell in the negative. There is an opposite side of the situation. We just fail to focus on it. The song performed by Garth Brooks, "The Dance," beacons us to live every moment to the fullest extent. Don't miss the dance; live life with no regrets.

I spoke with a friend whose death was imminent. As we joked about several things, she asked, "Why is everybody so quiet and moping around?" I replied, "It's the only side of the situation they see." She then laughed and said, "Oh, I guess I don't get to pass 'GO' and collect my $200!"

Where was her family and friend's focus? She wondered why they were already mourning even *before* her death. As I shared with her, "They are the ones not passing 'GO' and collecting $200. We already have ours and are spending it!"

Our life is a voyage of discovery. As long as you have your mind, you have something to offer. You just might have something to say or teach even in your last few hours.

A young boy, Jimmy, was dying with leukemia. His friend, Scott, sat with him one day as they played and told jokes. Scott laughed at the faces his dying friend was making as he impersonated an adult who had just been in the room. In fact, Scott laughed so hard he wet his pants. Then Jimmy began laughing hysterically, bent over, and holding his stomach. Gasping for air between laughs, his face bright red, his mouth open wide with no sound uttered, he looked as if he were in pain although quite the opposite.

"Oh my God!" his mother cried as she entered the room, thinking the worst. Jimmy, still red-faced and eyes wet and puffy from laughing, told his mother what had happened. Obviously he did not die then. His friend, Scott, commented at the funeral, however, that it would have been better for him to die laughing that day than the way he died later in the hospital.

We are programmed to believe nothing good comes from death. Our mind only focuses on the negative. Unless the person has lived a long life, we focus on what they will never have the opportunity to do. Instead, we should look at what they did have, and how it positively impacted our lives. We should find peace in knowing they have transcended this physical plane into the next phase of their eternal journey.

The only positive side that people sometimes recognize at the death of the terminally ill is that they are relieved of their pain and suffering. A blessing has been granted. At this point, however, we are still focusing on the circumstances of death and missing the opportunity to feel gratitude for the life that was lived and to celebrate their transition into a new life of beauty and love, depending on their beliefs.

Maybe you or someone you know is terminally ill. The hope that somehow a cure or last minute healing will occur often continues to support the denial that death will actually occur. By no means am I suggesting you should deny the hope of a cure or should not pursue all the means available to you for a cure. The compassion we as humans have for one another will push us to explore and research until we do find cures.

So much has happened over the past several years in the advancement of curing cancer; and when we think we can see the light at the end of the tunnel, the grim reaper throws us another disease, HIV (AIDS).

Please get the facts about this disease. It is not just the gay community that is affected by it. Is there someone in your family infected with HIV? If this person is homosexual, maybe you never understood or agreed with that person's lifestyle. You may be mad, upset, thinking, "How could he (or she) put me through this horrible disease and death?" Many a family member has had thoughts such as these when the HIV takes control of their loved one. Please do not turn away from this person. Forget your differences and use this last opportunity to give of yourself to this person.

There was a time in my early adulthood that my personal life was a disaster due to my own choices. My mother came to me one day, and I braced myself for another lecture on how I should live my life. Instead she said, "I don't agree with what you are doing, but I want you to know I'm here for you, and I love you." She followed those words with a hug. To this day, that meant more to me than anything she could have said.

. . .

Repeat this affirmation aloud:
"I live always, in all ways, in grace, love, acceptance, and forgiveness!"

. . .

Hospice and other organizations have made tremendous impacts on the lives of terminally ill persons and their families. While giving the comfort and care available, they also assist in dealing with death. Hospice gives the terminally ill the opportunity to die with dignity; and in most cases, in a family atmosphere. The love and support includes help with whatever concerns or plans the families need to care for during the final months and weeks.

The Hospice Team
is privileged to enter your lives to offer:
Peace, when life is fragile;
Gentle guidance into the unknown;
A quiet presence,
A compassionate touch,
A listening ear,
A being – with for those who are suffering,
A caring when time is near.

We listen with our hearts,
We know caring begets caring,
We thank you for caring for us.
                                    Jan Fritz, R.N.

What is the positive side to terminal illness? We all are going to die; we just do not know when. Terminal illness gives us a schedule. If you knew you were going to die in three months, would tomorrow be different? For most people, yes.

A person with terminal illness has the advantage of time to get their life in order. While often it may only be a few weeks or months, urgency prevails. Why do we have to face terminal illness before we treat life as if we had no tomorrow? All the excuses, what ifs, and procrastination only rob you of having a full, abundant life with no regrets and no duties left undone. Roll the dice and advance with anticipation toward 'GO' and collect the $200. Share, laugh, go for the gusto! It has amazed me what people are willing to share and give to one another when death is knocking at the door.

Do not ask a terminally ill person what they feel or think unless you are ready for the truth. Terminal illness has the power to change many of our life-long programs. Men will be more emotional and open. Women and children will be rigorously honest about what they think and believe. We could all learn a lesson from that. I have often said, "Be as happy as you can and let others join you, because the only thing you are guaranteed is what you just had." Persons with terminal illness have the opportunity to look at life in this way.

This Moment
I may never see tomorrow;
> **there's no written guarantee,**
And things that happened yesterday
> **belong to history.**
I cannot predict the future,
> **and I cannot change the past.**
I have just the present moment;
> **I must treat it as my last.**

I must use this moment wisely
> **for it soon will pass away,**
And be lost to me forever
> **as a part of yesterday.**
I must exercise compassion,
> **help the fallen to their feet,**
Be a friend unto the friendless,
> **make an empty life complete.**

I must make this moment
> **precious for it will not come again,**
And I can never be content
> **with things that might have been.**
Kind words I fail to say this day
> **may ever be unsaid,**
For I know not how short may be
> **the path that lies ahead.**

The unkind things I do today
     may never be undone,
And friendships that I fail to win
     may nevermore be won.
I may not have another chance
     on bended knee to pray,
And thank my God with humble heart
     for giving me this day.

I may never see tomorrow,
     but this moment is my own.
It's mine to use or cast aside;
     the choice is mine, alone.
I have just this precious moment
     in the sunlight of today,
Where the dawning of tomorrow meets
     the dusk of yesterday.

                  Paul F. Barnett

     A person with a terminal illness has the advantage of time to get their life in order. What part of your life has been left undone? Treat life as if you had no tomorrows. Is terminal illness an awful way to die? Actually, it gives you the opportunity to choose to live life to its fullest until your last breath. To be able to make the best out of what seems to be the worst is a true gift. You are the only one who can make that choice. To die is not that bad – only if you never lived.

     Terminal illness offers the person the chance to make final choices. Do not dwell on what you could have, should have, and will not have. Instead, look at what you did, what you have, and how that can never be taken away. This is your life. Make a difference.

     Most families will tell you that because of the experience, their lives were changed. We tend to focus, however, on the negative ways their lives had to change. They will tell you, instead, how great it was to have the time to spend with that person and share their lives like they never had before.

If you know someone who is terminally ill; do not shy away. You could be missing one of the best opportunities you may ever have to be with that person. The experience will never be forgotten. Your words to each other and the time you share will grow more precious with the passage of time . . . just like good wine.

A true blessing awaits you when you choose to be with one who is dying. Mark Victor Hansen shared about the death of his dad, "My humble advice is to always, always share your love with your loved ones, and ask to be invited to that sacred transitional period where physical life transforms into spiritual life. Experiencing the process of death with one you love will take you into a bigger, more expansive dimension of beingness."

. . .

Repeat this affirmation aloud:
"I have no need to be strong because I am one with that which gives me strength. I now let go and let God who is my strength, strengthen me!"

. . .

Suicide
After jumping off a bridge in an attempted suicide, a man shared his thoughts during the experience, "I knew halfway down I'd made a mistake!"

For this discussion, we will define suicide as the taking of one's own life for reasons other than poor health. Euthanasia, voluntarily ending one's own life due to physical infirmities, is a philosophical and spiritual issue that is less difficult for families to deal with than the tragic news of a friend or loved one ending their life for nonphysical reasons.

When someone takes his or her own life, we try to understand the reasons why. Were they depressed? lonely? defeated? bankrupt? Most often there is only one reason, whatever the cause may be, and that is, "I can't continue on like this." We try to make sense of it but to no avail.

Margaret Bookman, R.N., M.S., describes the thoughts of her clients as follows: "Their life is one of darkness – blackness and pain, all of which overcome them to the point they feel their life has no meaning. The pain seems unbearable emotionally. They feel absolute hopelessness." She continues, "Unless you have been there, it is difficult to explain. There is nothing family or friends can do; they need professional help. They are not 'nuts' or 'crazy.' Depression is very misunderstood by most people."

The emotions of those left behind are mixed with disbelief ("How could someone as smart as he is do such a thing?"), anger ("She had no right to do this and leave me"), and guilt ("I should have done . . ."). Do not go there mentally. Remember you can control your thoughts. When a person takes his or her own life, that individual has lost touch with reality. In reality there is always hope; but suicide defeats reality.

Question your focus; search out and remember the moments you had with that person that were positive. You cannot bring the dead back to life. It happened; it is over. You are alive; do not bury yourself with them.

Perhaps you have considered suicide. A piece of wisdom from the book, *Illusions*, by Richard Bach, also the author of *Jonathan Livingston Seagull*, reads as follows:

"Here is a test to find whether your mission on earth is finished: If you're alive, it isn't."

. . .

Repeat this affirmation aloud:
"I release everyone and everything that and who I have allowed to hurt me, knowing they were only doing their best with what they knew at the time!"

. . .

Death of a Child

Cat Stevens sang a song titled "Cat's in the Cradle" about a child being born and growing up to become a man. For all children to have the opportunity to grow up healthy and to become adults who die of "old age" is every parent's desire. Unfortunately that is the reality of this physical world as we know it. Children do die. Furthermore, regardless of how old a person may be, if his or her parents are still alive, to the parents, a child has died.

We expect at some point in time to make final arrangements for our parents. We do not expect to make final arrangements for our children. We expect to comfort and cuddle a crying baby, not to be the one crying and needing comfort.

The age old question, "When does human life really begin?" leads us to another question for this discussion: "When do we recognize that death of a child occurred?" I have often wondered if anyone would have an abortion if they had held even a few week-old fetus in their hands. Because we cannot see the fetus, it is easy for some to believe there is not a life there. I have handled very premature fetuses to full term infants. In every case, my experience led me to believe there was life. For the purpose of this chapter, we will be referring to life and death as it occurs from conception.

Most often, the death of a child is unexpected. The impact is a parent's worst nightmare. As a parent, you tend to feel there is no way to work through this experience. The incompleteness of not being able to fully share your life with your child is ever haunting.

Remember that when death of a loved one occurs, your words to those grieving are very important. I would like to emphasize that in this section of the book because of the frequency I have heard the "wrong" things said, such as: "It's O.K., you can have another one." "Well, you still have your other children." "I know how you feel." "You're better off." "I guess you just weren't meant to be a mother."

If you are guilty of making these comments, congratulations! Upon doing so, you became a member of the "Read My Lips Club"! Regardless of the most sincere intentions, these comments are usually not received well. Out of courtesy, the recipient more than likely held back his or her true feelings about your comment; but believe me, these comments do more harm than good.

Trying to determine what to say is not easy. If you feel the need to say something, do not give your opinion or advice. The best response might be: "I'm sorry. Let me know if I can help you in any way." That's all you need to say. They will let you know if they need you. As awkward as it is for us not to say something, sometimes silence may be the best support you can offer. A hug will mean a lot. When you hold someone's hand, hold it a little longer or squeeze it gently. Your vibrations will let them know you share in their grief and support them. Your presence is enough; you do not necessarily have to say or do anything. By all means, in conversations, talk about moments you shared with the child.

How can we transform the death of a child into a good experience, a celebration? Let's begin our discussion with even the smallest ones who are premature or who never took a breath on their own or who were only a few weeks old. Unlike a service where the public would come to celebrate a life that was lived, a service for the "smallest ones" is one in which the mother and father, close family, and maybe a few friends would gather. Most families prefer a private service at a location suitable to the them rather than a public service.

In some cases, I have offered the parents a choice that may not be for everyone; however, those who have taken the offer have said that it was the greatest thing I could have done for them. I am referring to the need or desire to hold the baby or even take it home. When an infant dies, never being able to hold the child again is difficult for the mother, father, and family. While it is necessary for the funeral director to have the child for a period of time to embalm and prepare for viewing, I offer the family the option to either take the infant home, or I will bring it to their home. The parents should be allowed to do whatever they feel empowered to handle emotionally.

One couple shares their feelings about how important it is for parents to be empowered to make their own decisions, once all the options are presented to them: "As parents of newborns, late miscarriages, and infant deaths painfully realize, their children never came home – home to the nursery so lovingly decorated and the warmth and comfort of that imagined family life. It was great to have our baby boy home. It allowed us, grandparents, and friends to have more intimate, private visitation with him. It was a wonderful, healing experience. Know that you ultimately have control, within the law, to do what is best for you."

Some of you immediately say, "No way! I wouldn't want to do that." That's fine. It is your choice. Depending on your age, you may remember that years ago, the deceased was always taken back to the family's home to stay until the day of burial.

The infant was a very real part of the family's life. To celebrate their life, thoughts should focus on the joy and excitement experienced when planning for the baby, preparation of the room, the clothes, the bed, the toys. Remember child preparation classes . . . picking out names . . . the suspense of wondering if it was a boy or a girl . . . what it was like the first time the mother felt the baby move. As you think about it, you realize that this child was a very real part of the family's life although never to the fullest extent everyone dreamed of.

Once during a child's service, I heard a minister tell a personal story which was effective in transforming our feelings of loss into feelings of happiness. She told the story of her six-year-old son who had lots of toys; but every time he saw a puppy, he would beg for one. He did not care whether it was in the pet store or someone giving puppies away at the door of the supermarket. Every time he saw one, he begged to take it home.

She finally gave in. Oh happy days! She could not believe how happy her son was when he saw the puppy and realized it was his to keep. He carried the puppy with him everywhere. They even slept together. Much to her amusement, he named the puppy, "Dog." For several days the two were inseparable.

One day, only a week after receiving Dog, the boy came home, but Dog did not run to greet him. The boy ran all over the house looking for Dog, calling for him. When he found Dog, it looked as if he were sleeping. He ran over to hug his puppy, but Dog did not respond. He was not asleep; for some unknown reason, he was dead.

Tears began to flow down the little boys face as he picked up Dog. He sobbed as he carried the puppy to his mother and asked, "Why did Dog die? I loved Dog. He was my best friend. I don't want him to die." The boy's mother shared in his sorrow as they wept together, not knowing the answer to the question, "Why did Dog die?"

Later she became angry at herself thinking, "Why did I ever get that puppy? How could I put my little boy through this terrible ordeal?"

As she continued thinking, however, she suddenly realized what an abundance of joy and happiness Dog had brought into her son's life in only a few short days . . . joy unlike he had experienced before. She then helped her son remember all that Dog and he had shared together. They looked at the photos they had made of Dog's first day home, Dog's chewing bone, and the boy's chewed up sock that Dog had taken for his own. They realized as they continued talking and laughing about Dog that even though the puppy had only been apart of their life for a short while, the time they had was far better than to not have had Dog at all.

No other puppy could replace Dog. He was special and always would be. They cherished that brief experience of love that was shared. No matter how brief, it was better than none at all.

As the minister concluded this personal story, a smile came to her face as she wiped a tear away. Any life, even the smallest ones, provide invaluable memories for all to cherish.

Sometimes children die after we have spent a lot of time with them, nurturing them and watching them grow. Remember when she rolled over? sat up on her own? He crawled today. Look, he has a tooth. "Daddy" was her first word . . . stood up at the coffee table . . . first step . . . getting into everything . . . terrible 2's. Oh, how cute he is on his bike. Kindergarten.

Then . . . Oh my God, no! He was so young. Why? It's not fair. These things are supposed to happen to somebody else. Someone else's child is suppose to be the statistical data for child mortality rates – not mine!

When our children die in their adolescent and teenage years, it certainly is not any easier. Whether the child is six months old, six years old, or sixteen, the experience brings pain beyond measure coupled with questions that will never be answered. We can choose to dwell on the loss, the guilt, the anger; or we can choose to move on. Do not forget, but remember. Because the childhood years are so full of changes, you will find yourself sharing more pictures and memories than if that person had lived to be 100. To dwell on how the death occurred or what you and your child were denied is not what they were about. Remembering what you had together, what you did, and what you shared will always be a better choice.

Remember when you thought the phone had grown attached to her ear? "Can I borrow the keys, Dad?" The prom. The communication gap. "I'm so proud of you." Focus on those memories or else the death will seem overwhelming as you ride the seesaw back and forth with your emotions. Ask for and accept support. You will need encouragement at this point to choose thoughts and emotions that reflect gratitude and joy for the life lived and to celebrate those memories.

To be a good parent is to lead to the best of your ability, to accept change, to know you are not always right, to love unconditionally. Remember not the worst but the best of your experiences. If death comes to haunt you, let your child's life live on through you. By doing so, your child's life will be honored. Do not bury yourself with them.

The following story is shared by a mother whose baby died a few months after birth. She describes her experience of saying "goodbye" and celebrating the life of her baby daughter:

"Planning what I felt was good for me and my family was a priority for me. Someone was bound to disagree as opinions go. In retrospect, I still feel in my heart the experience was releasing. In the farewell of my baby's short life, funeral and religious traditions plagued me. I directed my emotional uproar into prayer, asking my Creator and my baby's spirit to guide me in love.

"Mark offered me options I would never have dreamed of in my grieving process. Through all the details, it all seemed to fall into place, uplifting me and healing me. It was a celebration of life that some might label "breaking the rules." Yet, no one else shared the loving bond my baby and I felt.

Losing a child less than a year old is an unbearable pain at moments. I knew in my heart the suffering physically had ended for her. The world she went to was full of euphoric bliss. My previous experience with death and funerals was weary and dark. This time, however, I learned it can be a celebration of life. Though people may think a child that never spoke words hasn't lived in fullness. Yet I know my baby taught many every moment of her sickly life.

"I made decisions thoughtfully, as I selected the music for the service which reflected our time together. I spoke about our shared life to those who attended. In lieu of flowers, money was donated to a children's fund. I asked that bright colors be worn to the service, because she loved them so.

"It was her life – her celebration. I fought against the frigid traditions in order to make it personal, integrating some aspects out of respect for family members. I decided her life was not dark, ugly, sullen, and morbid. It was full of happy laughter, love, and music. Why should that change now?

"I asked her to work through me to make it healing. I allowed close family and friends to hold her little body at the calling hours. Her body was a sacred house which her spirit once dwelled within. For some people, grieving begins when they see the body and spirit are no longer one. I was the only person to hold her as the last light dimmed, and I heard her last breath. Others needed to share in the grief . . . people she loved. As they held her, the love poured out along with the tears of loss. Sacred moments . . . ones I would never change.

"There was one more day left until her body was taken away from me. Having her at home had been comforting to me – to hold her hands, cradle her, caress her hair, sing to her, and cry my tears of pain. She lay in the crib with her favorite blanket and toys, warmed I felt, as I slept on the floor. She was not in a dark room, a strange place, in a box. I could ease myself into releasing the physical attachment, my family could do the same.

"Loving her with all my soul, I wanted her in a familiar place. I took care of her everyday of her life here. Who was the best to care for her until the last moments? Just because her body was lifeless did not mean I needed to rid myself of her immediately.

"Those were moments of final touches of healing. Death scares me no longer. A lifeless body is not evil, I chose to keep her – a sacred creation. Holding her helped me to make the plans a celebration and healing.

"When the music played that I'd sung to her, it was our hearts singing together. As everyone talked about her after the service, it made the transition easier of now living with her in spirit. It was time to let her body go. Wherever she was, it was a better place. I knew I did the "right" things for me. The memories of keeping her until the last second I will cherish, so will others. She was a very happy baby; her life was not sad and cold. And when she came into my dreams that week and told me she loved me in spoken words, I knew in my heart it was right."

Jesus said, "Let the little children come to me, and do not hinder them, for the kingdom of heaven belongs to such as these." Matthew 19:14.

Know that they are safe and happy, surrounded by beauty and love in abundance beyond our imagination, protected from any pain, suffering, and hurt known to this world. Celebrate their uniqueness, innocence, and eternal happiness. Thank you, God.

. . .

Repeat this affirmation aloud:
"I know and believe my child's soul to be living in God's endless dream. My child is surrounded by love."

. . .

Chapter 8

Through a Child's Eyes

Growing up in a family whose life centered around the funeral business was an experience unlike most children's. I feel this gave me a rare insight to life that few have the chance to see. A so-called "normal childhood" is not one of playing "hide and seek" in a funeral home or one where seeing dead people is an everyday occurrence.

When I was a child, filling out forms that ask who to contact in case of an emergency was so easy. I always wrote in the funeral home number and address – which might have looked strange if someone did not know me. But afterall, who better to call? Someone was always there to answer the phone!

I am thankful for my childhood experiences and my parents' openness about death. For most of my childhood, we actually lived adjacent to the funeral home. It was always open for families to visit any time of the day or night; the doors were never locked. Even the embalming room (prep area) was open range for me. My father often would have a difficult time working because of all my questions – hundreds of them! One answer would only bring on another question then another. Finally someone would take me (or rescue him) to do something fun or to get ice cream.

Because of the openness of my father and the others working there, I never had nightmares or a fear of the dead and any part of the business. Our dinner conversations always included discussions of who died, when their funerals were scheduled, and so forth. Through my innocent eyes as a child, death was not a scary horrible thing from which to run to try to hide.

So why do children so often view death and the funeral home in such a negative way? Remember, children are influenced by their environment and the people they are around. Although my childhood environment was unique, the openness about death as a natural part of life can be duplicated in any home. Communicating to children and being honest about death is very important.

When a person dies that a child knew, you cannot (and should not) avoid telling them. Their curiosity will bring them to ask you or someone else about it. Children sense or know when something is not right. To keep them away or to avoid letting them be involved in every way is not the answer. For you to avoid communicating to the child will only allow the child to imagine his or her own ideas about what is happening.

Here are the "don'ts!" *Do not* say the deceased went away. The child will then feel abandoned, confused, and possibly guilty, wondering what he or she did to cause the person to go away. *Do not* say that the deceased is asleep. This may cause the child to wonder when he goes to sleep if he will end up like "so and so" in the casket. While dead people might look as if they are asleep, it is not a good answer to give. Be honest; tell the child the person is dead; explain the cause of death. If the question "Why?" is asked, refer back to the cause of death. Children generally will continue with one question after another; and at some point, you may not know the answer. Do not feel as if you must know all the answers. Be truthful and tell them you do not know.

Often you can remind children of the times they might have had a pet die. Remind them of the good times spent with the pet. Explain that although the person they knew is now dead, that does not mean they have to or will ever forget that person. Their experiences with that loved one will always be a part of their lives.

Only explain to a child what he or she is able to understand, using simple explanations and stories with which they are able to relate. One such story is the caterpillar that became a butterfly: "There was a caterpillar that built his cocoon. The other caterpillars could no longer see him and thought he had died. In reality, however, he had changed into a beautiful butterfly and was flying high above the other caterpillars. They did not see him because they had their heads down looking at the ground."

It is not unusual for a child under the age of seven to ask over and over again, "Where's Grandma?" even though you have told them that Grandma died. This is because a child this age has not yet developed the ability to understand the permanence of death. So, parents or caretakers, be prepared and do not let their questions upset you.

Depending on the age, allow the child to be a part of making some of the decisions and participating in the service. Encourage them to talk about the person and what they remember about him or her. Encourage the child to place something of their own with the deceased that expresses their good memories of that person – a drawing, card, or poem.

I feel strongly that children should be given the opportunity to view the deceased. This helps them accept that the person is dead and the way in which they knew and related to that person is now gone. They accept death of a loved one more easily by being a part of what is going on than to be shielded from it and left in confusion.

When cremation is the choice for final disposition, make sure the child understands what is being done and affirm with them that the body was only a "house" or a "tent" for the person who had lived there. Share with the child how we all change from our existing physical bodies but will still be the same person (spirit) we have always been. When a person dies, then the spirit (who they really are) has left the physical body behind to continue its eternal journey or adventure.

Remember that your response to death is a role model for children. Examine your thoughts and feelings prior to sharing with them. Be truthful above all else when talking with them; be ready to answer a lot of questions. Let your funeral director help you. I have taken children on a tour of the funeral home and shared with them what I did; and believe me, they have questions. At the same time, this removes the doubts, and they sense a feeling of comfort after seeing the facility.

When small children attend a service, do not try to keep them still and quiet. Ask someone who the child knows to be ready to take the child out to walk or play when he or she gets restless. Often an older child's participation in the service, such as sharing a story or poem about the deceased, will bring a delightful and meaningful moment for all. Know that many times a child also will have something to say that is valuable to them, and through sharing, to others as well.

From a child's point of view, adults make funerals a negative experience. If you do not believe me, just turn one loose in a funeral home and watch them. From a child's point of view, life goes on.

. . .

Repeat this affirmation aloud:
"I am, today, a person in a child's world. Curiosity
is my door to knowledge. There is nothing from
which I need to hide. I live for what life has to
offer."

. . .

Chapter 9
Choosing a Funeral Director

What is my idea of a good funeral director? Depending on where you live, you may refer to this person also as the undertaker or the mortician – yes, the skinny man in the dark suit and top hat such as you see in movies and on television, hanging around waiting for someone to die or measuring people for their caskets. People say I do not look like a funeral director. I thank them. We are, however, people just like you.

While I doubt you will find one person that can fill all of the ideals that follow, you should highlight the ones that are the most important to you and seek out that person if possible. Do not decide too hastily on a funeral home or a director. The ideal funeral director for you and your family will depend on several personal factors. Do not accept the phone sale or pre-planning sales call until you consider the options available to you. The person you choose must be adaptable. He or she is the one you will entrust your body and loved ones to. Is this person the one you want when you are in need? Can he or she be a caregiver and be genuinely sensitive to your needs?

You will not have a second chance to choose a funeral director. Whatever he does will remain forever so. While most are sympathetic and understanding, remember that this person is not a saint nor more of a sinner than others. He or she is an average person performing a job few can. Choose your funeral director as carefully as you would a doctor, lawyer, accountant, or any other professional. Many of the same factors should be considered.

You may be thinking, "I live in a small town and only have one or two funeral homes/mortuaries to choose from." I would suggest that after reading this book and completing the section, "My Funeral: The Celebration," make an appointment with the funeral director and discuss with him or her your wishes. If you are not satisfied that he or she will accommodate your desires, try to find another funeral director. Many are stuck in the old and only paradigms they know. When you and others show them what you need and desire, eventually the industry will change.

(I remember when my grandparents got upset with my father wearing a colored shirt instead of the traditional black suit and white shirt. That was a major concern to them although now it is totally acceptable. My grandparents would "roll over in their graves" if they could see how funerals have changed.)

Your funeral director should be someone you know. If not, make several visits with the person so you will feel comfortable with him or her, even comfortable enough to invite him or her to your home for dinner. After all, it makes sense to become a acquainted with your funeral director. It is not as if you know when you will need his services.

Find out if the person can accept changes and help you with all the details of the service. The director should handle service details such as obtaining the death certificate and appropriate burial/cremation permits as well as contacting the person officiating the service and/or recommend someone. I have even conducted the services myself for families who wanted that option.

He or she should offer to make arrangements with the cemetery and/or crematory, florist, musicians, and anyone else involved with the service. Transportation needs might be included if making airline arrangements are necessary for the deceased and family. Many directors will tell you to contact your own travel agent; however, you do not need the added hassle. Ask your director to do it for you if you wish. (Be sure your director is aware that the bereavement fare offered by most airlines may not necessarily be the lowest available.)

Other details include sending the obituary information to the newspapers and notifying the local media as appropriate; setting up memorial contribution funds; making arrangements for food, if needed; securing the location for the service; attractively arranging the items for the service (flowers, photos, etc.); completing Social Security forms and Veteran's forms; assisting with any insurance forms. In some cases, families also have special needs such as prohibiting particular individuals from entrance to the funeral home and service, to protect them from any distractions during this time.

The funeral director should offer to handle payment of all the cash items for you, such as honorariums to ministers and musicians, paper notices, airline tickets, services provided by other funeral homes, cemetery fees, and flowers. Of course, you will have to pay them back but at no additional fees for doing so.

When choosing your funeral director, make sure he or she does not insist on doing things a certain way, although you should consider his or her suggestions for the service and how to accomplish what you want. Do you trust this person? Does he or she respect your financial decisions and desires for the arrangements?

The funeral director should be willing to take the time to explain everything to you, including the differences between caskets, vaults, and all charges on your bill. He or she should never try to sell you expensive merchandise and tell you that this is how you can make up for feelings of regret or guilt over the loved one's death. If anyone ever tells you that you should spend more or buy a better casket, leave immediately! That person is not looking out for your needs.

Essentially, the funeral director is there to serve

you. He or she should be your number one support,
willing to help you in any way. Never hesitate to call
your director about anything that you may need or be
concerned about – even if you think it is silly to have
to ask.

The most important concern when choosing a
funeral director is knowing that he or she is caring for your
loved one in a respectful manner. When a family entrusts
the funeral director with one of their most precious posses-
sions, his or her conduct around the deceased should be
as respectful as if the family were present. On the
lighter side, I have often told families that I treat the
dead with special care because when I die, I do not want to
walk through the "pearly gates of heaven" and have all
those I have cared for saying, "There's that (blankety
blank) that did that to me!"

Perhaps funeral directors are, for the most part,
responsible for the existing ways in which we deal
with the death of our loved ones. They have become
accustomed to certain ways of counseling survivors and
caring for the deceased that would be difficult for them
to break out of.

Some changes have occurred through the years;
but so often, funeral directors handle arrangements
the same as always. For example, a funeral director will
probably lead you to make the same arrangements for
your father's funeral as your mother's, although hers was
years ago, without ascertaining whether such a service
would be appropriate for your father and for you at this
time. Likewise, funeral directors often fail to adjust facets
of the funeral to meet your particular needs. They have
a routine that everyone seems to fall into. Remember,
however, every death is an individual experience.

Your funeral director may not be comfortable with
some of the ideas and changes you choose to have as a
result of reading this book. You may hesitate because of

his or her resistance. The results I have witnessed first-hand, however, convinced me of the value of taking the positive approach. I encourage you to push your director to adapt to your desires.

Being a third-generation funeral director, I have known many in this profession, from east to west. With only a few, rare exceptions, you can have confidence in knowing that the members of this profession are good, sincere, and honest people with a genuine desire to serve the community to the best of their abilities. Most will be willing to help you in whatever way you desire to make the arrangements and service a memorable celebration – celebrating the life that was lived as well as your transition into the next phase of your eternal journey.

Chapter 10
To View Or Not To View

"Why on earth would anyone want to see a dead person?" is one of the comments most often made in conversations concerning death and dying. This chapter will provide you with opinions and options for "viewing" the deceased, as we refer to it in the funeral profession. The main reason for viewing the deceased is that only a few people can truly accept the fact that such an event has occurred without actually witnessing it themselves. Some excuse themselves from viewing by saying that they wish to remember the deceased as he or she appeared when they were alive. Viewing the deceased, however, can be one of the biggest and most helpful steps in accepting the death and dealing with it.

As you read on, you will see how strongly I feel on this subject. I think every family member and close friend should at least be given the opportunity to view the deceased. Some are afraid it will be a painful experience. It can, on the other hand, be helpful and comforting. Many families have expressed to me how beneficial the viewing opportunity was to them. Contrary to beliefs held in certain parts of the country, viewing can leave a peaceful, loving, beautiful memory of the deceased, especially if the last time you saw them was unpleasant.

I know people who for one reason or another did not have the opportunity to see their loved ones after death occurred. To this day, some of those individuals are still hoping and believing somehow that their loved ones are still alive. This occurrence over and over again has reinforced my belief that close family and friends, not necessarily the general public, should view the deceased in order to accept the fact of that person's death. Personally, I am not a proponent of viewing the deceased during or after the funeral service.

While viewing is generally considered to be part of a traditional burial-type service, it can and does serve a very important purpose for survivors, regardless of the type of service arrangements – burial or cremation. We are in a constant evolution of change. Our ideas about death and the type of service people choose today are not exempt from changes. In certain regions, now more than ever, people are choosing cremation rather than a casket burial.

Some funeral directors do not consider cremation as a valid choice. They consider it a trend, thinking it will not last. I believe it is not a trend and deserves recognition by funeral professionals as a viable choice. Even if it is a trend, those that choose cremation deserve the same rights, service, and options as those who chose a casket burial.

There are some professionals – funeral directors, psychiatrists, ministers – as well as some families who disagree with the choice of cremation and memorial service (or a service with the body absent). They argue that this "substitution" is unacceptable because it is often held several days to even weeks after the death occurred and emotions are not as intense. They feel strongly that a body should be present and many feel that the casket should be open.

I have found cremation to be the choice of many people as a reaction to their past experiences of attending funerals where the deceased was present in a casket and often viewed during the service. These individuals, and perhaps yourself, decided at that moment that they did not want anyone looking at them when they were dead. "Just cremate me," they thought.

With the new concept, however, a private viewing may be held prior to the service if desired, then photos and personal items are displayed at the service rather than the deceased body, focusing on and celebrating the life of that person. Most ministers would agree that viewing of the deceased should not be the final part of a service, but it is important. When viewing is chosen, I highly recommend it be done prior to the service. Use the time during the service to focus on celebrating the life lived and journey forward.

In the case of cremation or when the deceased body is not going to be presented for a scheduled viewing period, ask your funeral director to prepare the deceased with minimum preparation for private viewing by close family and friends. This preparation should include bathing, disinfecting, setting the facial features (closing eyes and mouth), and dressing the body.

This type of viewing would require only a portable table or stretcher. It is not necessary to purchase an alternate container or a casket for viewing unless desired. An "alternate container" usually refers to a casket-shaped cardboard or pressed wood box that has less decorative interior and exterior and is only suitable for use during cremation. Personally, I recommend the cot as better suited for this type of private viewing. Some funeral directors offer rental caskets for viewing; but once again, look at your needs and don't feel pressured to rent or buy anything. Be sure to ask what you will be charged, if anything, for any part of this service rendered to view the deceased.

The viewing should last only for a brief period, generally a few minutes to no longer than a couple of hours. Most of the families I have served have taken less than thirty minutes. I always offer families and friends a time of privacy. This may be the time that a person needs to express some of the thoughts that are on their mind. Generally people will take this time to say their good-byes or even to place notes, poems, and momentos with the deceased. Upon request, these items are often buried or cremated with their loved ones. Do not hesitate to ask for a few minutes alone if you desire.

Note that for a service which includes public viewing or in a case where family and close friends cannot view within 24 hours of death, it normally is necessary to embalm the body. What is embalming? It is the artificial preservation of a dead body. Embalming serves three purposes: restoration, preservation, and sanitation.

Restoration maintains the life-like appearance and removes the deterioration and scars caused by disease and accidents. Preservation, probably the least important of the three, preserves the body, in some cases, hundreds of years. Sanitation is of utmost importance because people come into contact with the body either through touch or airborne exposure. Embalming is a method of eliminating the pathogens that cause disease.

By the way, let me remove some myths regarding embalming brought to my attention by questions that have been asked of me. The body is never hung up or treated in the manner of a meat packing plant. Bones are not broken. Rigormortis is removed not by force but by simple flexing and rotating the area affected. The body is not cut open from head to toe (not to be confused with an autopsy). Usually, a small two-inch incision is made to perform the fluid injection process. No body parts are removed.

Please ask prior to viewing what you should expect to see. Each person's body reacts somewhat differently to the effects of death. Discoloration occurs and sometimes distortion is caused by swelling. This could make the viewing experience negative instead of fulfilling the needs and purpose intended. If the funeral director recommends embalming, trust his or her professional opinion. Even then, embalming is not always a solution to viewing problems; and unfortunately, may in some cases contribute to problems.

In that situation, I always ask the family to tell me someone they trust who can be sensitive to their needs. Then this person is asked to view the deceased and decide if the family should proceed with viewing. Surprisingly enough, there have been times when I was concerned about the appearance of the deceased, but others thought he or she looked fine. So when in doubt, I recommend getting the opinion of a third party who knows the family.

In cases where death has occurred in an accident, the family or friends may have seen the deceased at the time of death or shortly thereafter in the emergency room. The deceased, more times than not, had tubes and other devices attached to them that were used in the life saving attempt. In these cases, a special viewing time later will give the family and friends the opportunity to view in a more peaceful atmosphere and help erase the often unpleasant picture left in their minds at the time of death.

Many families have been forever grateful for the skillful embalmer who was able to modify or erase the scars of violence or ravages of disease. Shortly after graduating from mortuary college, I embalmed a man, taking great care to do my best. Afterall, my dad had the reputation of being the "best" embalmer ever in that area. I had a great teacher in him and felt confident in my own skills at that point.

As the wife of the man came in for viewing, she became extremely upset upon seeing him. She kept asking me what I had done, exclaiming this was not her husband! "He doesn't look right," she cried.

My dad put his arm around her and said, "It's O.K., I'll take care of it."

The wife went back to the lounge area and my father and I wheeled the casket back into the prep room. I asked, somewhat hurt and embarrassed, "What are you going to do?"

He replied, "Nothing, you did a great job. He looks fine – just watch."

So for about five minutes I stood and waited in total confusion. Then we wheeled the man back into the room, unchanged. The wife approached the casket and said, "Oh, thank you. He looks so much better. I'm O.K., now."

More times than I care to say, I have had suicide cases where "everybody and their dog" showed up for the viewing, some because of the drama and curiosity surrounding the circumstances. Often I would put a little extra makeup or wax on an area on their head so the curiosity-seekers would think that was the spot the deceased shot himself. People would even ask me about the spot. I loved to be able to say, "Nope, try again." Does that sound mean? I don't think so. I just don't have a lot of time for nosy gossips!

While most people will say they do not want to remember the deceased as they would view them at a funeral home, it very well could be better than the last time they saw the deceased. This decision, however, is a personal one for you to make – not one for others to make for you. So many times, in an effort to help you with decisions, well-meaning people will persuade you in the direction that they would choose. Make sure it is your decision. I hate to hear people say, "I think it's for their own good," when they have not even asked the person for their thoughts or feelings regarding the subject.

Viewing the deceased can be an emotional experience but a helpful and rewarding one. As long as you can accept the death and move on, viewing may not be necessary. Most importantly, be true to yourself, very few of us can do this. Some people are simply afraid to look at a dead person or would rather not. However, the decision not to view often causes doubt and regrets, wondering if the "right" decision was made. I know this much for certain, after the deceased is cremated or buried, it is too late to change your mind.

Here is a true story I would like to share that is on

the lighter side of the subject. Years ago in Tennessee, my cousin, who was about eight years old, was visiting our grandparents who actually lived at the funeral home. As kids, we always felt free to wander around the building. That particular day, there was a family there for a viewing period who was known to have frequent "fainting spells" when at the funeral home. When one fainted, it would be like a domino effect around the room, one after another.

As my cousin strolled through the rooms of the funeral home, he came upon the room where this family was viewing the deceased. He saw one of the family members faint, then another . . . several fell before the domino effect ended. Not understanding what had happened, he ran as fast as he could to the office where my Dad was standing. Breathless, he shouted to my Dad, "Uncle Millard, Uncle Millard, get up there quick. There are dead'uns laying all over the place!"

Contrary to popular belief, promoting the idea of "viewing" is not the act of devious morticians thinking of ways to make more money. If we were to take a hard look at it, the expense of restoration and preparation of the deceased, with the preparation room, equipment, supplies, training, and hours involved, probably is never recovered by the charges you are billed.

At a viewing recently, the event was more like a celebration, with everyone putting cash in the casket. I noticed this and inquired of the reason. They said it was for the benefit of the deceased in the next life, to help him get a fresh start. By the end of the night there was $1500 cash in the casket. I was so impressed with the idea, that I took the cash and doubled the $1500 by replacing it with a check for $3000. (Just kidding!)

Chapter 11
What Will It Cost?

The fact that the final care of our loved ones is a business is unfortunate. I have often wished the business or financial side could be somehow separated from the care side. Talking about money at this time in a family's life feels cold and harsh.

The financial aspects of death, however, are important. This book would not be complete without touching on the subject of final expenses. Every time I see or hear the media give the "average" cost of a funeral, I wonder what families think when often their statement for services is two to three times more.

As you know, the "average" is influenced by the very lowest numbers to the very highest numbers. In most cases, it will be around $6,000. Depending upon where you live, however, this figure is often misleading the same as the average cost of a house can be drastically different depending upon your location.

Some people will come to me and share their experience of price shopping for a casket or the service. However, comparing only casket prices or any other singular costs can be extremely misleading in this industry – so much so that you could still end up paying more. Look at the total price for all the arrangements, services, and merchandise. Funeral homes will offer a general price list, a casket price list, and an outer burial container (vault) price list. In almost every case, each funeral home will have different prices for each of the items. So at any one funeral home, you may spend less for one item but pay more for another item.

For example, Funeral Home A charges $1200 for casket #B32 whereas Funeral Home B charges $895 for the same casket. Funeral Home B would appear to be the least expensive. If you look further, however, Funeral Home B's

charges from the general price list for your services amount to $3400 whereas the same services at Funeral Home A are $2895. Therefore, Funeral Home A is truly the least expensive.

If you were dealing with only merchandise such as the casket, pricing would be easier. A casket, however, may represent only a small percentage of the total funeral bill. Often the bottom line for your final expenses will be close to the same if you shop for comparison.

People have often asked me, "Why is one funeral home more or less expensive for the same merchandise and services?" Of approximately 22,000 funeral homes in the United States, almost every one is different somewhat in their pricing. Like any other business, overhead is generally the main factor coupled with the number of services they have each year to cover those expenses.

To look at price only can be a mistake. The facility, the transportation (hearse, family car), the location, and the personal service you receive from the staff should all be considered. One funeral home may be less expensive but use a stationwagon or van for a hearse while another may have a $60,000 hearse such as you may desire.

I am not advocating that you should spend more or choose one facility over another because they have a more expensive building or rolling stock. We all live differently and have different desires. Your decision is going to be based partially on your choices of appearance and comfort. This can be very important. After all, a funeral is not like a wedding. There's no dress rehearsal. So choose a funeral home in which you will be confident in the service and comfortable with the facility. Think of it as if you were renting the facilities and vehicles and hiring the personnel from the time that death occurs to the burial or cremation.

So what are the costs? I could not give you a realistic figure without being in your location and without knowing the type of services and merchandise you desire. I can only encourage you to make an appointment with a funeral director to begin pre-planning. Go ahead and call that person. It may be your first time to make such an appointment, but they do it every day and will welcome the opportunity to help you.

Pre-planning will not only be a final gift to give to your loved ones, it will also save you money. Of course, funeral expenses have gone up over the years as has everything else. I can remember when $600 was a nice funeral – and I am not that old!

If you decide to have a casket burial, you will then choose a casket and maybe an outer enclosure. Caskets come in many different styles, colors, and prices. While construction varies, they all serve the same purpose. Basically there are only two types: protective and non-protective.

A protective casket is designed to resist the entrance of air and water after being sealed and buried. They are made from materials such as bronze, copper, or steel. The steel varies in thickness which affects the price of the casket. The least expensive to the most expensive generally goes from 20 gauge, 19 gauge, 18 gauge, 16 gauge, stainless steel, copper, and bronze.

Non-protective caskets may be constructed of wood or steel. Steel offers metal construction but the sealing mechanism does not resist the entrance of air and water. Wood caskets offer choices of mahogany, cherry, oak, poplar, pine, and veneer or pressed wood. Personally, I have found wood offers a warmer and more natural feeling than steel. I have found most people choose a casket based on the appeal or their finances with less concern about construction or quality of craftsmanship. While it is true that a copper or bronze casket may be more resistant to corrosion and a 16 gauge is heavier and thicker than a 20 gauge, your decision should be based on what you like best and fits your budget.

An outer enclosure is a receptacle to put over or to place the casket into. Many cemeteries require these. There are basically two types: sealing and non-sealing. Grave liners (non-sealing) made of concrete, fiberglass, plastic, or wood serve to keep the dirt and its weight from damaging the casket. Without a grave liner or vault, the weight of heavy equipment used for digging and maintenance would possibly cause a grave to collapse.

Vaults (sealing) are made of the same materials as liners (except wood) with the addition of steel. Vaults may seal in a couple of ways, either by an airseal or a mechanical type.

You will only see the vault or liner for a few minutes, but if the appearance is important, you will probably have to spend more on this item. Basically, the function and purpose of the outer enclosure is not in its appearance. Keep this in mind and do not be misled. From reading my example, you know that I choose a Wilbert SST vault. It is strictly my personal choice. There are several vaults that are just as good in quality.

Like my grandfather and father, I believe the outer enclosure is more important than the casket. The casket's purpose is for appearance; the enclosure's purpose is for protection. It is all based on personal preferences.

What about clothing? Some funeral homes offer a price list for clothing or it may be part of their general price list. Clothing is a personal choice. You may use clothing which belonged to the deceased, or you may pick something from the funeral home's selection. Some families shop for new clothing.

I have always felt it was better to use clothing that you were accustomed to seeing the person wear, rather than possibly a suit they wore only on special occasions. I have heard people say, "All dressed up and no place to go," or "They look better in these clothes than they ever did while alive." Remember, this is the person you have known. This is probably not the time to try to change them.

By the way, if you bring clothing to the funeral home, be sure and include everything they normally wore, including undergarments, socks, etc. (Shoes are optional, although the cowboy usually wants his boots on.) So many families forget the underclothes!

Once I had a widow give me a strange request. She wanted her husband buried without any clothing from the waist down. Why? Only she and her funeral director will ever know for sure!

Because you have taken the responsibility to choose your services and merchandise now, you have the advantage of several options:

Option 1: Buy a paid-up insurance policy or one that fits your financial needs that will increase in value (to keep up with inflation) to cover the costs. You also could put the money in a C.D. (certificate of deposit) or a similar investment that would carry no penalty for death withdrawal; but generally, insurance will pay a higher rate of interest and allow you to make payments.

Option 2: Purchase a plan through the funeral home of your choice. This type of plan will cost the amount of their current charges and should be guaranteed not to cost you any more than that amount, regardless of the date death occurs. Confirm this guarantee, along with the ability to transfer the plan anywhere without losing the interest accumulated. Of course, if you transfer the plan to another funeral home, the charges may vary, in which case you will be responsible for the difference. It would be rare not to find the same or similar services and merchandise at other funeral homes. Sometimes the problem is that the interest does not transfer. Be sure to check out that part of the plan.

Make allowances for cash advance items, such as flowers, death certificate copies, etc. This is often overlooked or omitted when paying for such a plan; then later, surviving family members do not understand why there are more charges to pay. The price of cash advance items cannot be guaranteed, but it is better to allow for them.

Many funeral homes offer great plans; but unfortunately, some are not worth the paper they are written on. Always seek advice from other family members or an attorney before making a decision as to the credibility of the plan. Also confirm that the total funds would be available for use when death occurs.

With either option, you should add 10-15% to the amount to cover any additional items you may not anticipate. The extra money might help a member of the family with travel arrangements or might be used for transportation and other necessary services if you were to die outside of the area you have chosen for your final arrangements.

Option 3: Choose your services and merchandise and take the chance of having the financial resources to cover the expenses when the time comes. Pre-planning does not require pre-payment. However, pre-paying and knowing the financial affairs are in order is deserving of serious consideration.

In Options 1 and 2, the money is not considered a part of your assets for the purpose of Medicaid. The pre-payment you make can be done properly prior to applying for Medicaid assistance.

The movie *Love Story* made popular the phrase: "Love means never having to say you're sorry." Love is giving everyone your best so much so that there is never a reason for regrets. Unfortunately, I can not begin to count the number of times I have helped surviving family members make decisions about arrangements and financial obligations when the overwhelming feeling in the room, if expressed, would be something like, "How could (the deceased) have left us with this burden if he or she really loved us?" A lot of deceased, if they could, would have to say, "I'm sorry."

Well, if you don't get it by now, you probably won't until it is too late! Maybe tomorrow? How do you know you have a tomorrow? Just do it. Your final gift . . .

"If it is to be; it's up to me."

Chapter 12

My Example: "A Dance with Life"

A celebration that honors the memory of your life can be arranged and conducted by your survivors. On the other hand, I feel it is far better for you to take the responsibility of making your final arrangements – either general or detailed. This chapter is my own celebration plan – my final gift to my loved ones. Perhaps you can see from my own plans how I have incorporated the new concept.

After reading my plan, I encourage you to discuss your ideas with your loved ones. It is the final gift you can give to your family. While some may think it to be sad or even sick, it can be enjoyable and satisfying. Do not think of it as your funeral but as your celebration.

At this point in my life, I choose burial instead of cremation. I would opt for cremation, however, should the circumstances of my death cause mutilation to my body.

I want to be buried beside my wife in the cemetary we have chosen (oh, yea – I forgot she is probably going to out-live me!). I want a mahogany or cherry hardwood casket with a Wilbert S.S.T. vault. I would prefer to wear a sport coat and slacks with a casual shirt or sweater – no neck tie! Anyone in my family who desires should have the opportunity to view my body the night before my service. This can be done at the funeral home.

I would prefer to have the burial at 10:00 or 11:00 a.m. the next day – not any earlier. I would hate for people to have to get up early for my service. This would be only for family and close friends.

While most people would have the committal (burial) after the funeral or celebration service, I believe it is better to have it prior to the service. This is contrary to tradition, but it makes more sense. Why spend all the time in the funeral service comforting the family, healing the hurt and loss, celebrating the contributions of the life lived, only to go to the cemetery and be reminded of the finality and your last contact with the deceased! I have literally had to pull people off the casket at the cemetery and out of the grave because they were so upset. Do not put yourself through this process. Allow the funeral or memorial service to serve the purpose for which it was created. End the day by remembering and celebrating.

Greatness
A man is as great
As the dreams he dreams,
As great as the love he bears,
As great as the values he redeems,
As the happiness he shares.

A man is as great
As the thought he thinks,
As the worth he has attained,
As the fountains at which his spirit drinks,
As the insight he has gained.

A man is as great
As the truth he speaks,
As great as the help he gives,
As great as the destiny he seeks,
As great as the life he lives.

> *No greater life could I have*
> *had because of those whom*
> *I have loved.*

Thanks, Mark

At the burial, I would like the preceding poem read, "Greatness" with my addition and also the poem, "God's Promise."

God's Promise
God hath not promised
Skies always blue,
Flower-strewn pathways
All our lives through.
Sun without rain,
Joy without sorrow,
Peace without pain.

But God hath promised
Strength for the day.
Rest for the labor,
Light for the way.
Grace for the trials,
Help from above,
Unfailing sympathy
Undying love.
                              Author Unknown

The closing prayer would be as follows:

Lord, Mark walks with you, for this we know.
What we see is his body empty from what we knew,
he lives, even greater than before.
We thank you God for that to come of which we
cannot see.
Through Jesus Christ we pray, Amen.

Now, it is time for a celebration! Following the burial, in the afternoon, I want a memorial celebration to be held anywhere suitable for my family and friends. At the celebration I would like photos of my life displayed at the front of the room or meeting area, along with my golf bag and clubs, something from my scuba gear, my fly fishing rod, my saxophone, an eagle sculpture, my Bible, a copy of this book, an arrangement of wild flowers, and anything else that my family feels is significant in my life.

At the front door or entrance, I want my Harley Davidson motorcycle parked and the memory photo board displayed.

For the thirty minutes prior to the service, I want some of my favorite music played, such as "Sax by the Fire," the John Tesh Project, C.D. selections 1, 2, 8, 9, 11; "Up on the Roof," by James Taylor; and "Morning Has Broken," sung by Cat Stevens.

The order of the service can be determined by my family and the person officiating, but I want the service to begin by playing "Amazing Grace," the bagpipe version. At some point thereafter, I would like "Memories" from Cats played, followed by three to five of my friends and/or family members sharing special moments they had with me.

The person officiating should speak about my life and significant events thereof. Scripture passages that I want read include Ecclesiastes 3:1-8, 12-13. I also would like "The Dance" by Garth Brooks played. I would also like a video or slides showing photos of my life to be shown with one of my favorite songs played in the background, Brian Ferry's "Dance with Life."

After a closing prayer, I want the song "Celebrate" played as everyone is leaving.

Following the memorial celebration, I want everyone invited to go to my home or a place of my family's choice for a cookout of burgers and hot dogs . . . and at dark, FIREWORKS! I want people to enjoy themselves, laughing, dancing, and making toasts to life in my memory – knowing that I died happy because I lived every day as if it were my last!

By now you either think I am one of the weirdest people in the world or maybe a person with some insights about how to live and die. Remember, there is a better way to deal with death than we have been conditioned to believe. While not all families I have worked with use my ideas to their fullest extent, the following is an example of one who adapted the ideas to their own situation:

Bill and Cathy came in with questions about pre-arrangements. Both seemed to be a picture of health. Bill, however, had only a few months to live. Acceptance of his pending death was truly a struggle for Cathy. "He's so young," she thought.

We spent some time getting to know each other. As we talked about Bill's final wishes, he began to feel comfortable knowing his desires would be met. I shared my ideas and feelings about a memorial celebration. Not having attended such a service before, their interest and curiosity brought about further questions. From that discussion, the celebration was planned:

"Gone Fishing"

At Bill's death, I met with Cathy and she gathered the photos and items for Bill's service. Bill was a fly fishing guide and loved the sport. Cathy shared, "I was somewhat puzzled when Mark asked me to gather the fly fishing items as to how he was going to use them. When I arrived at the memorial service, I was overwhelmed. He had captured Bill's life by the display in the room. My friends were amazed. Although I had been upset about Bill's death, the service and manner his life was reflected gave me a sense of his accomplishments and what his life meant to everyone."

"Mark turned an undesirable situation into a pleasing experience, focusing on the life rather than his death. While I would prefer to have Bill with me still, I am content to know death can be thought of in a different

manner than I had ever realized."
 Like the wind which carries one ship east and
another west, you can lift yourself up or pull yourself down
according to the way you set your sails of thought:

If you think you are beaten, you are,
If you think you dare not, you don't.
If you like to win, but you think you can't,
It is almost certain you won't.

If you think you'll lose, you're lost,
For out in the world we find,
Success begins with a fellow's will –
It's all in the state of mind.

If you think you are outclassed, you are,
You've got to think high to rise,
You've got to be sure of yourself before
You can ever win a prize.

Life's battles don't always go
To the stronger or faster man,
But soon or late the man who wins
Is the man WHO THINKS HE CAN!

Chapter 13

Your Plan: "The Celebration of Life"

This chapter or workbook is here to help you plan your own arrangements and celebration service – the final gift to your loved ones. The vital information worksheet includes all the information needed by the funeral home for the death certificate and appropriate permits required by the law. The celebration worksheets will help you plan your celebration service. Refer to the Appendix where forms are included should you want to become familiar with the forms used by funeral homes when making arrangements.

I encourage you not to procrastinate. No matter what your age or health, now is the best time.

IN CELEBRATION OF

_____

(your name)

I. Special Moments in My Life I Would Like Shared:

_____
_____
_____
_____
_____
_____
_____
_____
_____
_____
_____

II. Personal Items Which Might Be Included in a
Celebration Display of My Life (Include items from work,
hobbies, interests, personal items you treasured such as a
special book, hat, trophy, photo.)

_____
_____
_____
_____
_____
_____
_____
_____
_____
_____

III. Special Poems, Scripture, or Prose I Want Read:

_____
_____
_____
_____
_____
_____
_____
_____
_____

IV. Music That I Want Played or Sung:

_____
_____
_____
_____
_____
_____
_____
_____
_____

V. Other Suggestions:

_____
_____
_____
_____
_____
_____
_____
_____
_____

APPENDIX

Funeral Instructions

The following information is for guidance at the time of my death. It is intended to assist those handling my personal affairs. I have expressed my preferences on certain subjects which, unless changed by unexpected circumstances, I hereby desire and request.

1. I wish my services to be held at _____

2. I would prefer as clergyman _____

3. I request the following music _____

4. My funeral director is _____

5. I have viewed caskets and would prefer _____

_____

6. Outer enclosure desired _____

7. Clothing preferred _____

8. I desire my funeral expenses to total approximately $ _____

9. I prefer: ❑ Burial ❑ Entombment ❑ Cremation

   Cemetery _____

   Grave No. _____ Lot _____ Section _____ Block _____

10. My executor/executrix is _____

11. Special instructions _____

_____

_____

WITNESSES: Signed: _____

_____   Print Name _____

_____   Date Signed _____

VITAL STATISTICAL AND BIOGRAPHICAL RECORD

Full Name _____

Address _____

City & State _____ Phone _____

Marital Status _____ Spouse _____

Birthplace _____ Birthdate _____

Father's Name _____ His Birthplace _____

Mother's Maiden Name _____ Her Birthplace _____

Length of Residence Here _____ Coming From _____

Usual Occupation _____

Employer _____ Education (Yrs.) _____

Social Security Number _____ Veteran _____

Religion _____ Church _____

Clubs, Organizations, etc. _____

_____

_____

_____

Remarks _____

_____

_____

_____

PERSONS TO BE NOTIFIED

Relationship:	Name:	Address:

FUNERAL PURCHASE AGREEMENT

Name of Deceased _____ Last Address _____ Date of Death __ / __ / __

Charge to _____ Telephone No. _____ Date of Service __ / __ / __

Buyer's Home Address _____ City _____ State _____ Zip Code _____

Charges are only for these items that are used. If we are required by law to use any items, we will explain in writing below. If you selected a funeral which required embalming, such as a funeral with viewing, you may have to pay for embalming. You do not have to pay for embalming you did not approve if you selected arrangements such as direct cremation or immediate burial. If we charged for embalming, we will explain why below.

A. CHARGE FOR SERVICES SELECTED:

1. Professional Services
   Services of
   Funeral Director / Staff .... $ _____
   Embalming .... $ _____
   Other preparations of body .... $ _____
   $ _____

2. Facilities and Equipment
   Use of facilities for viewing
   (Visitation / Wake) .... $ _____
   Use of facilities for funeral
   ceremony .... $ _____
   Other use of facilities .... $ _____
   $ _____

3. Automotive Equipment
   Transfer of remains to
   funeral home.......................... $ _____
   Hearse .... $ _____
   Limousine(s) .... $ _____
   Use of other
   Automotive equipment .... $ _____
   $ _____

4. Other services / facilities / equipment
   _____ $ _____
   _____ $ _____
   TOTAL OF SERVICES SELECT .... $ _____

B. CHARGES FOR MERCHANDISE SELECTED:

Casket / other receptacle .... $ _____
Acknowledgement cards .... $ _____
Register book(s) .... $ _____
Memory folders / prayer cards .... $ _____
Temporary marker .... $ _____
Clothing .... $ _____
Other clothing .... $ _____
Cremation urn .... $ _____
$ _____
TOTAL OF MERCHANDISE SELECTED .... $ _____

C. SPECIAL CHARGES:

forwarding of remains to
_____ $ _____
Funeral home / mortuary
Receiving of remains from
_____ $ _____
funeral home / mortuary
_____ $ _____
Immediate burial .... $ _____
Direct Cremation .... $ _____
TOTAL OF SPECIAL CHARGES .... $ _____

D. CASH ADVANCED:

Cemetery charges .... $ _____
Lot and Deed .... $ _____
$ _____
Removal .... $ _____
Clergy honorarium .... $ _____
Organist / Singer .... $ _____
Flowers .... $ _____
Newspapers .... $ _____
Certified copies of death certificates
_____ at $ _____ each ..... $ _____
Cards of Thanks .... $ _____
Vault Service .... $ _____
Marker .... $ _____
$ _____
$ _____
TOTAL CASH ADVANCED................ $ _____

SUMMARY OF CHARGES:

A. Services................................. $ _____
B. Merchandise .... $ _____
C. Special Charges .... $ _____
D. Cash Advances .... $ _____
TOTAL OF ALL SELECTIONS .... $ _____
(Balance Due)................................
$ _____

Reason for embalming _____
_____

Cemetery or crematory requirements, if any _____
_____

Charges are only for those items that are used. If the type of funeral selected requires extra items, you will explain the reasons in writing on this contract.

In the event I wish to question any area of your service, I may contact you at my convenience at (XYZ Funeral Home).

METHOD OF PAYMENT:

Less: ❑ Cash Received on Account .... $ _____
❑ Sums consisting of my assignment to you of the proceeds
of _____
_____
(type of benefit assigned) Which I am making this day in a separate instrument .... $ _____

I agree that any monies assigned above shall be paid to you within 30 days of the date of this contract. Upon your giving me at least five (5) days prior written notice that any monies due under the assignments(s) described above have not been paid to you as promised, you can require that any such unpaid amount(s) previously credited to my account be paid by me at once.

UNPAID BALANCE DUE BY _____, 19 _____ $ _____

TERMS: The balance due is payable upon completion of the services, however, no finance charge will be added for a minimum of 30 days after which a FINANCE CHARGE of 1 1/2% per month (ANNUAL PERCENTAGE RATE 18%) will be added to the debt or any portion thereof on the last day of each month. If this agreement is placed in the hands of an attorney for collection. I (we) agree to pay attorney's fees.

WARRANTIES: The only warranties, express or implied, granted in connection with goods sold with this funeral service are the express written warranties, if any extended by the manufacturers thereof. No other warranties and no warranties of merchantibility or fitness for a particular purpose are extended by seller. By his (her) signature, buyer(s) in addition to authorizing seller to conduct the funeral, perform the service, furnish the materials, and incur the charges specified within this agreement, on the terms and conditions set forth, acknowledges that prior to the execution of this agreement, a printed or typewritten list of retail price of the funeral services and funeral merchandise offered by seller was made available to buyer(s).

Executed this _____ day of _____, 19 _____   Signature (1) _____
                                                                                                Buyer
ACCEPTED FOR SELLER:

By: _____   Signature (2) _____
Signature of Licensed Funeral Director   Co-Buyer, if any

GENERAL PRICE LIST

These prices are effective as of:

The goods and services shown below are those we can provide to our customers. You may choose only the items you desire. However, any funeral arrangements you select will include a charge for our basic services and overhead. If legal or other requirements mean you must buy any items you did not specifically ask for, we will explain the reason in writing on the statement we provide describing the funeral goods and services you selected.

BASIC SERVICES OF FUNERAL DIRECTOR
AND STAFF .... $

Our fee for the services of funeral director and staff includes, but is not limited to, staff to respond to initial request for service; arrangement conference with family or responsible party; arrangement of funeral; preparation and filing of necessary authorizations and permits; recording vital statistics; preparation and placement of obituary notices; staff assistance prior to, during and following the funeral, including coordination with those providing other portions of the funeral, e.g. cemetery, crematory and others. Also included in these charges are overhead expenses relative to our facility such as insurance, maintenance and utility expenses, secretarial and administrative cost, and equipment and inventory costs.

This fee for our basic services and overhead will be added to the total cost of the funeral arrangements you select. (This fee is already included in our charges for direct cremations, immediate burials, and forwarding or receiving remains.)

EMBALMING .... $
Except in certain special cases, embalming is not required by law. Embalming may be necessary, however, if you select certain funeral arrangements, such as a funeral with viewing. If you do not want embalming, you usually have the right to choose an arrangement that does not require you to pay for it, such as direct cremation or immediate burial.

OTHER PREPARATION OF BODY
Includes cosmetology, hairdressing,
dressing and casketing .... $
.... $
.... $
.... $

USE OF FACILITIES AND STAFF
FOR VIEWING/VISITATION .... $
Our services include set-up of visitation area, placement of encased remains, display of floral arrangements, supervision of and attendance during the visitation. (Charge per day)

USE OF FACILITIES AND STAFF
FOR FUNERAL CEREMONY .... $
Our services include coordinating the funeral arrangements, supervision of funeral, and staff to attend funeral ceremony.

USE OF FACILITIES AND STAFF
FOR MEMORIAL SERVICE .... $
Our services include coordinating the memorial service arrangements, supervision of the memorial service, and staff to attend the service.

USE OF EQUIPMENT AND STAFF
FOR GRAVESIDE SERVICE .... $
Our services include accompaniment of remains to cemetery, supervision of graveside service, and staff to attend service.

USE OF EQUIPMENT AND STAFF
FOR CHURCH SERVICE .... $
Our services include coordinating the funeral arrangements, supervision of funeral, and staff to attend funeral ceremony.

TRANSFER OF REMAINS
TO FUNERAL HOME .... $

Beyond   miles, add $ per mile.

HEARSE (Casket coach) .... $
Beyond   miles, add $ per mile.
LIMOUSINE .... $
Beyond   miles, add $ per mile.
SEDAN .... $
Beyond   miles, add $ per mile.
SERVICE/UTILITY VEHICLE .... $
Beyond   miles, add $ per mile.

CASKET .... $ to $
A complete price list will be provided at the funeral home.
OUTER BURIAL CONTAINER .. $ to $
A complete price list will be provided at the funeral home.
MISCELLANEOUS MERCHANDISE
CREMATION URNS .... $ to $
AIR TRAY .... $
ACKNOWLEDGEMENT CARDS
Type A - per twenty-five .... $
Type B - per twenty-five .... $
REGISTER BOOK(S)
Type A - (each) .... $
Type B - (each) .... $
MEMORY CARDS .... $
PRAYER CARDS .... $
.... $
.... $
.... $

FORWARD REMAINS TO ANOTHER FUNERAL HOME
This charge includes removal of remains, necessary services of funeral director and staff, embalming, necessary authorizations, and local transportation to airport.
A. With minimum shipping container .... $
B. With casket selected from our funeral home (in addition to the cost of the casket) .... $
C. Air Tray .... $

RECEIVING OF REMAINS FROM ANOTHER
FUNERAL HOME .... $
This charge includes temporary shelter of remains, transportation of remains to cemetery, and necessary services of funeral director and staff.

IMMEDIATE BURIALS .... $ to $
Our charge for an immediate burial, without any attendant rites or ceremonies, includes removal and shelter of remains, local transportation to the cemetery, necessary services of funeral director and staff, and authorizations.

A. Immediate burial with casket provided
by purchaser .... $
B. Immediate burial with:
.... $
C. Immediate burial with casket selected from our
funeral home (in addition to cost of casket) .... $

DIRECT CREMATION .... $ to $
Our charge for a direct cremation without any attendant rites or ceremonies includes removal of remains, local transportation to crematory, necessary services of funeral director and staff, and authorizations. If you want to arrange a direct cremation, you can use an alternative container. Alternative containers encase the body and can be made of materials like fiberboard or composition materials (with or without covering). The containers we provide are (specify containers):

....
A. Direct cremation with container provided
by purchaser .... $
B. Direct cremation with alternative container .... $
C. Direct cremation with casket selected from our
funeral home (in addition to cost of casket) .... $

DISCLAIMER OF WARRANTIES
RELATING TO THE ARRANGEMENTS OF

_____

THIS FUNERAL HOME MAKES NO WARRANTIES OR REPRESENTATIONS CONCERNING PRODUCTS SOLD FOR THE SERVICES FOR THE ABOVE-NAMED DECEDENT. THE ONLY WARRANTIES, EXPRESSED OR IMPLIED, GRANTED IN CONNECTION WITH THE PRODUCTS SOLD WITH THIS FUNERAL SERVICE, ARE THE EXPRESSED WRITTEN WARRANTIES, IF ANY, EXTENDED BY THE MANUFACTURERS THEREOF. THIS FUNERAL HOME HEREBY EXPRESSLY DISCLAIMS ALL WARRANTIES, EXPRESSED OR IMPLIED, RELATING TO ALL SUCH PRODUCTS, INCLUDING, BUT NOT LIMITED TO, THE IMPLIED WARRANTIES OF MERCHANTABILITY AND FITNESS FOR A PARTICULAR PURPOSE.

By my signature below, I acknowledge receipt of the original copy of this document.

Signed _____

Date _____

To order additional copies of this book call 1-800-871-9715
or write to PO Box 773897 Steamboat Springs, CO 80477

NOTES

_____
_____
_____
_____
_____
_____
_____
_____
_____
_____
_____
_____
_____
_____
_____
_____
_____
_____
_____
_____
_____
_____
_____